EMAIL
MARKETING
FOR
AUTHORS

DALE L. ROBERTS

Email Marketing for Authors: Grow an Email List that Actually Sells Books

Disclaimer
The information provided in this book is accurate to the best of the author's knowledge at the time of publication. However, because of the evolving nature of the topics discussed, some information may change over time. The author makes no representations or warranties regarding the accuracy or completeness of the information contained within this book. It is the reader's responsibility to verify any facts or details, and to conduct further research or consult updated sources as needed.

Some recommended links in this book are part of affiliate programs. If you purchase a product through one of the links, then I get a portion of each sale. It doesn't affect your cost and greatly helps support the cause. If you have any reservations about buying a product through my affiliate link, then Google a direct link and bypass the affiliate link.

TABLE OF CONTENTS

WANT A PROVEN PATH TO A STRONG BOOK LAUNCH?

Get my free **Bestseller Book Launch Checklist** and weekly insider tips to help you sell more books.

Grab yours at

DaleLinks.com/Checklist

SELF PUBLISHING WITH DALE

INTRODUCTION: WHY EMAIL STILL WINS

Everything I know about email marketing, I learned from the relationship I have with my wife, Kelli. When we first met, our conversations were light and exploratory—testing the waters, seeing if we connected. But as our relationship grew, so did the depth of our trust and communication.

What I didn't realize at first was that building an email list—much like building a relationship—requires patience, intention, and trust.

Authors looking to sell more books and grow a massive platform must go the extra mile to build and deepen a connection with their readership. Otherwise, they're left at the mercy of algorithms or complete chance.

The one asset you truly own—no matter how favorable or dire the circumstance—is your email list. Having one gives you a distinct advantage over authors who rely solely on social media or retail sites to sell more books and reach their ideal readers. These services may be free to use, but they control the rules, limit your reach, and can disappear without notice. That's why your email list isn't just a tool; it's your safety net and foundation.

What's dangerous about relying on systems you don't control, like social media or online retailers, is that your access can disappear overnight. Whether you unknowingly violate a rule or the site itself goes under (RIP Vine, Mixer, MySpace), you could lose your direct line to readers. Even if recovery is possible, you'll waste time, sales, and momentum trying to rebuild.

Amazon holds complete control over your publishing account. One wrong move, even by accident, can result in permanent termination. I've shared in previous books the story of an author who earned six figures relying entirely on KDP Select. He didn't have a website, print editions, audiobooks, or an email list. When Amazon shut down his account, his entire presence disappeared. With no direct line to his readers, he had to rebuild from the ground up and hope they would find him again.

A solid email list safeguards your author business by creating a direct connection to your readers. By delivering value through email, you stay in control of your audience relationship. That connection can lead to more sales, deeper engagement, and steady business growth.

When I first broke into the publishing business in 2014, I didn't even know what an email list was. I soon discovered it was a collection of email addresses used by authors to send newsletters, promotions, or updates to subscribers. It seemed intimidating to me at first, especially when I learned that some authors had hundreds of thousands of email subscribers.

I couldn't fathom how anyone could even begin to accumulate that many when all I had were maybe a dozen people, all of whom were friends, family, and acquaintances.

I tried everything to get more subscribers, from begging on social media to beating up my current subscriber base to send more readers. Over my first year and a half of being in the business, I spun my wheels trying to gain any traction growing my email list.

That wasn't enough for me to throw in the towel. I knew I could make email marketing work; I just needed to study more and implement what I'd learned. I peeled through books, videos, and online courses, learning what I could.

I eventually sought guidance from someone who'd gone farther down the path. That mentorship helped me turn email marketing from an afterthought into a core pillar of my business. By applying what I learned and building on the foundation I already had, my list grew from a trickle to thousands of eager readers.

You won't find shady shortcuts or sketchy tactics in this book. No hacks, no Jedi mind tricks—just ethical strategies that build real trust with your readers. If you treat your subscribers with respect and deliver genuine value, they'll stick with you for the long haul.

Authors who consistently invest some time each week in their email list gain a lasting edge, one that compounds far beyond social media bursts or the whims of the algorithms.

In the pages ahead, you'll learn why email marketing is the single most effective tool for standing out in a crowded digital world—outperforming social media, blogs, and even author websites. You'll discover how to attract the right readers, repel the wrong ones, and build a strong foundation with systems that support long-term growth. I'll walk you through how to choose and manage your email service provider, craft high-value emails even when you're short on time, and grow a responsive list of readers who want to hear from you. You'll also learn how to analyze results, improve performance, and manage your list with confidence.

Anyone lacking the confidence to craft an email can lay their fears to rest, because I'm going to show you precisely how I produce high-quality emails even at a moment's notice and with little thought. All the while, you'll still deliver value and build trust with your subscriber base. Eventually, you'll realize how straightforward it can be to build a thriving list of loyal readers who can't wait to hear from you.

Finally, you'll learn how to analyze your email metrics such as open, click, and unsubscribe rates so you can make smarter decisions, improve performance, and ensure your messages continue reaching the readers who care most.

By the end of this book, you'll know exactly what to do and how to do it. Results will vary from one author to the next, but if you're making progress, even small steps forward, you're on the right track. I'm not saying you should coast through, but I'm also not encouraging the kind of burnout hustle I fell into early on. You'll learn how to strike a healthy balance so email marketing works with your writing, not against it.

If you take what you learn here, apply it right away, and build on that knowledge over time, you'll look back in a few years and recognize the massive impact it made on your life. You'll see exactly why I view email marketing as the digital equivalent of making friends and building a network of peers. Once you see your list through that lens, it becomes much easier to send your next email, launch your next project, or share something meaningful with your readers.

Let's dig in!

CHAPTER 1:

STOP CHASING EVERYONE AND START ATTRACTING THE RIGHT READERS

I remember exactly where I was when a friend pointed to my first book and asked, "Who is this even for?" The question hit me like a cold slap. Not because I didn't have an answer, but because I *thought* I did. That moment made me realize that I was writing for everyone, which meant I was speaking to no one at all.

The more dialed in you are with who your ideal reader is, the better you'll know the precise audience you want to attract onto your email list. Once you know your audience, you'll be able to provide them with exactly what they want in this two-way relationship.

Quality matters more than quantity in building a subscriber list. In my early days of email marketing, many of my peers had deep email lists. They flexed large numbers, seemingly bragging about how incredible they were at email marketing. However, when pressed for open and click rates, they gave me either radio silence or reported atrociously low stats.

A big email list doesn't always indicate an effective marketing strategy. If all you want is volume, you can find any shady service to boost your numbers and get thousands of email subscribers. That is not how you want to build your business, and it's a fast way to get added to a blacklist by various organizations that monitor online spam. You'll be dead in the water if your email or domain land on that list, so do yourself a favor: Don't buy subscribers and never acquire emails without the recipient's permission.

Every country has its own rules for email marketing, but two of the most widely enforced are the CAN-SPAM Act in the United States and GDPR in the European Union. These laws require you to get clear permission before contacting someone using an email address, and you must include an unsubscribe link in every message. The penalties for breaking these rules can be serious, so don't mess around. Follow the law, protect your readers' privacy, and build your list the right way.

Let's assume you're following the rules and only communicating with subscribers who want to hear from you. How do you attract more of those subscribers who want to see your email in their inbox? Knowing your audience puts you in a better position because you know exactly how to communicate with them and precisely what they want. They'll naturally want to check out your emails and learn more about what you have going on in your world. This relationship lets you share information that is helpful to your publishing business, and your readers will get what they need because they are interested in what you have to share.

Well-curated email lists will see better results in so many ways, but one important metric is higher open rates. Greater open rates lead to lower likelihood of landing in spam folders or on any dreaded online blacklist. Let's talk more about how to attract the right subscribers to your list.

DEFINE THE PURPOSE OF YOUR EMAIL LIST

An email list can play many vital functions in an author business, including:

- Driving book sales
- Promoting new releases
- Building a reader community
- Gathering early feedback
- Sharing valuable and relevant content
- Cross-promoting with other authors

Knowing precisely what you want from your email list is critical, because you need to feel personally invested in it. You shouldn't build a list just because someone like me or another author says you should. Do you want more book sales? Would you like to get early reader feedback or to build an advance reader copy team (ARC)? Or are you looking to work with other authors to grow together?

You're welcome to think big and expect bigger from your list, but you can't do that without first knowing what you want. Prolific indie author and self-publishing expert Craig Martelle shared in an interview how he doesn't build an ARC team drawing from his email subscribers.[i] With a large email list in the tens of thousands, Craig didn't see the purpose in giving away free copies of his book for reviews. The fact is, his readership will leave reviews without the promise of advance access, so using his email list for building an ARC team doesn't make sense for him.

Knowing what you want from your email list is the first step to building it. After all, if you don't know why you're emailing your readers, then every one-time broadcast, like a newsletter or update, becomes noise instead of a real connection. You'll send inconsistent content, attract and keep the wrong subscribers, and struggle to measure what's working. Without a clear purpose, your email list turns into a leaky bucket—full of effort with nothing to show for it.

Your email marketing strategy will change over time and evolve. For instance, you might not agree with how Craig uses his list now; maybe you want more reviews by having an ARC team for your next book launch. That's okay!

> *Side note: A soft launch refers to a gradual and low-key introduction of a new book or project to a limited audience before a wider release. Authors can test the waters, gather feedback, and create buzz without the pressure of a full-scale launch.*

No author's career follows the same path, so it's important to consider your reasons for email marketing in the first place. This understanding will help guide what you do and how you communicate with your subscriber base.

What is driving you to build an email list today? Are you nurturing superfans, selling books, or building long-term relationships? It's okay to want all of these, but I want you to commit to one specific focus as a starting point so that it'll be much easier for you to draft every broadcast.

GENRE, VOICE, AND READER EXPECTATIONS

Reader expectations play a crucial role in how you communicate. Take this lightly, and you'll see your subscriber base dwindle down to nothing. Get it right, and you'll see excellent subscriber retention and continued list growth through consistent promotion.

Genre makes a huge difference in the tone and frequency of your emails. Different genres and niches have distinct tones that resonate best with readers. A romance author might write with warmth and intimacy, while a thriller writer may favor a more suspenseful and urgent tone. Fantasy fans might like whimsical and imaginative language, while nonfiction readers could prefer something more straightforward and professional.

Let's not ignore your needs though. The tone you choose should align with your brand and the emotional reaction you want to evoke from your audience. Email marketing isn't about pretending to be someone you aren't. You don't have to fake it till you make it; be authentic and lead with your best self every time. I always think before I send an email:

Does this email represent me in the best possible way?

I carefully review every word and link in an email before hitting send. Typos and grammar mistakes matter, but what counts more is making the message clear, professional, and worth reading. Mistakes can happen. One or two minor errors won't ruin your reputation, but sloppy, rushed writing will. If you're asking readers to invest time and trust in you, your emails should reflect the same care you put into your books.

What sets you apart from the other emails in a crowded inbox is your unique voice. Embrace it! You will always attract and keep the right subscribers when you're being your truest self.

One of the most common questions in email marketing is how often you should contact your subscribers. This depends on audience expectations. Some genres, like self-help, may thrive on frequent updates, reflecting the audience's need for answers and solutions to their problems. Others, like sci-fi horror, might benefit from less frequent emails.

Regardless of genre, focus on what your subscriber base prefers. Do they like to have one email per week? Or do they thrive on three or more broadcasts? If you're not sure, ask. Your email subscribers will appreciate having a say in how often you appear in their inbox. Asking puts them in the driver's seat so that they're more invested in what you have to share from one week to the next.

The type of content you write can also dictate frequency. Serial fiction authors might send chapters regularly, while authors with standalone novels might opt for less frequent, more substantial newsletters. It's been my experience that nonfiction readers appreciate more frequent emails and fiction readers can skate by with one email every week or even every month.

COMMON MISTAKES THAT KILL LIST QUALITY

The quality of your subscriber base far outweighs the quantity. After all, which would you rather have:

- an email list of 100,000 subscribers with 1% opening your emails
- an email list of 10,000 subscribers with a 50% open rate

It's simple math. The large list boasts 1,000 content-consuming subscribers. The much smaller list has 5,000 people who engage with your email. The first list is great to brag about, but the second list carries more weight based on its higher engagement.

Building an email list shouldn't be solely about subscriber numbers. Getting email subscribers is the simple part. Keeping them engaged over the long haul is hard. You will lose subscribers; it's inevitable. Don't personalize unsubscribes. Life gets in the way, or people lose interest and want to move on to other things. When you lose one email subscriber, remember that there are thousands who'll willingly replace that one inactive or disengaged reader.

The metrics that matter most center on subscriber engagement, not just how many people are on your list. We'll dig deeper into that soon. Yes, having a much larger list is nice and makes life easier, but only if you have people on your list who truly look forward to your content.

Even though I already touched on how you can easily buy subscribers through shady services, there are other means that can be nearly as ineffective. For instance, you will find many promotional services that offer list-building services through giveaways. This option might include giving away a free book to someone who subscribes using their email address.

The problem with list-building this way is that you're attracting a readership who are going to expect you to deliver more stuff like the freebie. When you ask them to buy a book, they might be less apt to grab a copy since they have to part ways with more than their time. There's nothing inherently wrong with this practice, but it's not as effective as it once was.

Free giveaways can draw in a lot of new subscribers, but the drop-off and disconnect will happen once the fuzzy feelings of receiving a free ebook have subsided. Now, the reader faces opening your emails and they're being asked to open their wallets to get your book. (Gasp!) Giveaway campaigns are effective in drawing in new subscribers, but they can also provide fleeting success since the subscriber base is often less invested in your content over time.

Consider why giveaways attract both ideal and less than ideal readers. When someone grabs a book for free, they're usually not thinking about building a relationship. They just want the freebie. But downloading a book and reading it are two *very* different things. Some readers stop at the download, which means your lead magnet ends up forgotten on their device.

That's not to say that giveaways are all bad, but be prepared to see a massive reduction in subscribers who stay or remain engaged for the long haul.

You'll see that you're attracting the wrong readers by looking at engagement rates, unsubscribe stats, and bounce reports. Low open and click rates may suggest disinterest, while high unsubscribe rates indicate that your content isn't aligning with reader expectations. Also, negative feedback is a key sign of a disconnect. If you ever get an email response from a disgruntled subscriber, you'll know you either didn't deliver on your promise or the reader is in the wrong place.

If you're pulling in the wrong crowd, it's time to reassess. Start by digging into your subscriber data. Find out who is opening, clicking, and sticking around. Then tighten up your messaging and promotions so you're speaking to the *right* people, not just anyone with an email address.

Make sure your content speaks directly to your ideal reader. Segment your list and customize your emails so each group gets what matters most to them. From time to time, run an engagement campaign or simply ask what your audience wants.

Above all else, stay true to your voice. The right people will show up and stick around when your message feels real, intentional, and worth their time.

CHAPTER 2:

LEAD MAGNETS THAT ACTUALLY WORK

uthors can build an email list with a simple call to action in their book, on their site, on social media, and anywhere else. Well-written books can attract readers to your email newsletter, but the pace will likely be slow. To expand your subscriber list, give your readers an offer they can't refuse.

Enter the lead magnet.

Also known as a reader magnet or bribe, the lead magnet is an enticing offer designed to attract subscribers, such as a free ebook, short story, or exclusive content. You provide that valuable content in exchange for receiving your reader's contact info. Lead magnets are great for nurturing relationships and converting subscribers into loyal fans and long-term customers.

WHAT MAKES A LEAD MAGNET WORTH SUBSCRIBING FOR?

It's not enough for you to simply offer any old lead magnet. What you choose should be deliberate and reader-focused. Start with your ideal reader in mind and ask yourself these questions:

1. **Does it help the reader?** A strong reader magnet solves a real problem, satisfies curiosity, or gives your audience something they already want. If it's not useful or interesting to your ideal reader, it's simply filler and fluff.

2. **Is it on-brand?** The tone, design, and content should feel like an extension of your books and author voice. A mismatched freebie might bring in the wrong crowd and confuse the readers you want.

3. **Will it grow your list?** Readers will provide their email addresses only if your offer is compelling enough. If it doesn't spark instant interest, it won't get traction.

4. **Is it different from what's already out there?** If your magnet looks and sounds like every other freebie in your genre, it'll get lost in the noise. Make it stand out with a fresh angle, format, or promise.

5. **Can you get it in front of people?** Even the best reader magnet won't work if no one sees it. You'll need a simple promotion plan, whether that's using links in your books, banners on your site, or regular mentions on social.

6. **What happens after they opt in?** A magnet is a handshake. What matters is how you follow up, deliver value, build trust, and set the tone for the rest of your email relationship.

If your reader magnet has these qualities, it's more than a list-building tool. It's the start of a meaningful relationship. The tricky part is identifying the right content that'll coax your ideal audience to join your email newsletter.

Start with source content. For instance, I pulled in thousands of emails for my fitness brand newsletter with the lead magnet *Top 10 Fitness Tools to Lose Weight*. I created a three-page report in less than a half hour with Microsoft Word. Later, I created a one-page PDF through Canva for a subsequent lead magnet that drew in even more subscribers: *The 4-Minute Fat-Burning Home Workout Plan*. These two lead magnets alone drew in tens of thousands of engaged subscribers from my various books like *The 90-Day Home Workout Plan* or *An Ultimate Home Workout Plan Bundle*.

For nonfiction authors, think about your reader's biggest problems and how you can provide a solution.

Before you hand out your reader magnet, make sure you have a smooth delivery system in place. Most email platforms don't host your lead magnet, so you'll need to upload the file to cloud storage, like Google Drive or Dropbox, and link to it in your welcome email. If you go this route, double-check your share settings. Give view-only access to a PDF version of the file and make sure no one can edit or access anything else in the folder. You don't want someone tampering with your content or stumbling onto unrelated files. Some platforms, like Kit, will host your lead magnet for you, so you can upload it directly and skip the extra steps. Either way, keep the download process quick, simple, and secure for your reader.

Don't overcomplicate the offer with too many moving parts. The content I published showed that my target audience craved specifics on effective weight loss equipment and quick workouts. Both reader magnets delivered on all six of the questions I asked myself about my audience's needs.

I've found that less is more with nonfiction lead magnets. You'll want something that's easy to produce but invaluable for your reader. Here are a few suggestions worth considering:

1. **Checklists and Cheat Sheets**: Pull the most actionable steps from your book and put them into a clean, easy-to-use format they can keep handy.

2. **Printable Worksheets**: Help readers apply what you teach. Worksheets turn your ideas into action and make the content feel even more valuable.

3. **Resource Lists**: Save them time. Offer curated lists of tools, books, or websites that support the content of your book or area of expertise.

4. **Quizzes or Assessments**: Engage readers by helping them learn something about themselves. These work great for getting clicks and starting conversations.

5. **Email Course**: Deliver a multi-day email course that teaches one concept in small, digestible parts. Content delivery builds trust over time and keeps you top of mind.

These options are a sample of what you can do because you can also offer webinars or video tutorials, sample chapters or excerpts, infographics, exclusive interviews or case studies, and more. Test a couple of different lead magnet types to see what resonates most with your readers and drives more subscribers to your email list.

For fiction authors, choosing a lead magnet can seem tricky if you let yourself get overwhelmed with the possibilities. Much like nonfiction authors, what you offer needs to be dead simple to share and to create. A few examples of what you could offer your readers might include:

1. **Free Short Story or Novella**: If readers enjoy your writing, they'll want more. A short story or novella, especially one tied to a series or a beloved character, is one of the easiest and most effective ways to win your audience over and pull them deeper into your world.

2. **Exclusive Previews**: Give your readers a sneak peek into an upcoming book by providing a taste of what's to come. This offer works great if you place it at the end of a published book.

3. **Bonus Content**: Think alternate endings, deleted scenes, or extra chapters that add depth to the story they already love. This kind of content feels exclusive and makes readers feel like insiders.

4. **Character Backstories or Profiles**: Give readers a reason to care even more about your characters. A detailed backstory, journal entry, or mock interview can strengthen that emotional connection and keep them coming back for more.

5. **Behind-the-Scenes Extras**: Share your inspiration, your outlining method, or a fun anecdote from the writing process. This content makes you more relatable and your stories even more immersive.

Much like nonfiction, you're not limited to these few options. Consider other ideas like character profiles or backstories, themed activity or coloring books, a reader's guide or discussion questions for book clubs, thematic recipes or craft ideas, printable bookmarks and art, and so much more. Again, test out a few lead magnets to see what works best for you.

VALUE PROPOSITIONS THAT CONVERT

Having a great lead magnet is only part of the equation since now you have to frame your offer in a way that coaxes readers to part ways with their email addresses. Yes, you can get decent results from simple copy like:

Get the Bestseller Book Launch Checklist when you subscribe to my email newsletter at DaleLinks.com/Checklist.

To increase the likelihood of readers subscribing to your email newsletter, refine what you say and how you say it. Marketing copy is your solution since it's meant for promoting your brand, or, in this case, encouraging readers to subscribe to your newsletter.

Crafting effective marketing copy can feel overwhelming at first, but with practice and testing, you'll start to see what resonates. The key is knowing your audience—what they need, what they struggle with, and what they want. Communicate with those factors in mind, and your message will land.

Here's how you'll want to create marketing copy that converts:

1. **Compelling Headline**: Create a catchy and relevant headline that grabs attention and is easy to read at a quick glance.
2. **Clear Value Proposition**: You must clearly state what benefits the reader gets from subscribing and/or engaging with your offer.

3. **Strong Call to Action (CTA)**: Include a clear and persuasive CTA that tells readers exactly what to do next.

4. **Conciseness and Clarity**: Keep the marketing copy clear and to the point, avoiding jargon or unnecessary details while maintaining a friendly tone.

5. **A/B Testing**: Experiment with different versions of copy to see what resonates the most with your audience. You can create different marketing copy for the front and back matter of a book or anyplace else you plan to share your offer.

My previous example was okay, but I doubt it'd entice many readers to join my email newsletter. When we implement all the tips for high-converting marketing copy, we'll get the following:

READY TO LAUNCH YOUR BOOK THE RIGHT WAY?

Join over 10,000 authors who have used my **Bestseller Book Launch Checklist** to plan and execute successful launches.

Subscribe at DaleLinks.com/Checklist and get the checklist instantly. You'll also receive weekly publishing tips, platform updates, exclusive discounts, and real-world insights to help you thrive.

Don't launch blind. Grab your checklist now.

Since I'm never satisfied with one version of copy, I build something more in-depth that highlights all the benefits of getting my reader magnet while also showcasing what to expect from my email newsletter.

LAUNCHING A BOOK? DON'T WING IT.

Get the exact checklist thousands of authors have used to plan, prep, and launch bestselling books.

When you subscribe to my newsletter at <u>DaleLinks.com/ Checklist</u>, you'll get instant access to the **Bestseller Book Launch Checklist**—a simple, battle-tested tool used by over 10,000 indie authors to take the guesswork out of launching.

But that's simply the beginning.

As a subscriber, you'll also get my weekly-to-biweekly insider emails packed with:

- The latest self-publishing news and platform updates

- Exclusive discounts on trusted author tools

- Behind-the-scenes insights you won't find on YouTube

I've been in your shoes, and I know how overwhelming book marketing can feel. This checklist will give you structure. My emails will keep you sharp. And together, we'll turn your next book launch into something worth celebrating.

Don't launch blind.

Grab your checklist now: <u>DaleLinks.com/Checklist</u>

The same thing holds true for fiction authors, so let's improve this generic CTA:

Subscribe to my email newsletter to get the prequel to Infestate. *Find out the true origins of the bloodthirsty creatures that ravage the Westgate Fashion Mall.*

While the marketing copy isn't terrible, it's leaving out many vital elements for the reader to latch onto. One of the biggest burning questions from my fiction series is: Where did the otherworldly creatures come from? With that in mind, let's explore that pain point.

Short copy:

Want the truth they never find out in the series?

Grab *Infestate: Origins*—the exclusive prequel novella revealing where the creatures came from.

It's free when you join the email newsletter at DaleLewisRoberts.com/OriginStory.

Subscribers also get early access to new releases, exclusive discounts, special promos, and behind-the-scenes looks at Dale's twisted world of sci-fi horror.

No one in the series knows the origin.

You will.

Long copy:

The Origin of the Outbreak Was Never Meant to Be Discovered...

Infestate: Origins is the exclusive prequel to the award-winning sci-fi horror series *Infestate*.

It reveals what no one in the story ever learns—where the creatures came from.

This story is **not available anywhere else**.

It's free when you subscribe to the email newsletter.

Inside, you'll follow four strangers trapped in a boutique after hours. The mall goes silent. Then the screaming starts. The blood flows. And something hunts them from the other side of the grate.

But that's just the beginning.

As a subscriber, you'll also get:

- Early access to future stories and releases

- Exclusive discounts and subscriber-only promos

- Bonus content and lore from the *Infestate* universe

- Personal insights and updates from Dale's world of sci-fi horror

If you like *Alien*, *Dead Space*, or anything that keeps you up at night, you're in the right place.

Join the newsletter. Get *Origins*. Learn the truth.

> > > DaleLewisRoberts.com/Origins

Again, experiment with different marketing copy based on where readers will find this offer. For my fiction work, I use short copy in the front matter because most new readers don't care about the series origin. For the back matter, I slip in the long copy because after they have read the book, readers will be more invested and, most likely, salivating at the chance to uncover the mystery of where these creatures came from.

To identify where email subscribers are coming from, create unique trackable links. You can create a subdomain or subdirectory like:

1. **Subdirectory**: DaleLewisRoberts.com/Origins
2. **Subdomain**: Origins.DaleLewisRoberts.com

Pick up a domain name through any service like Namecheap or GoDaddy. From your domain host's dashboard, you can usually create a subdomain with a few clicks. If you're using WordPress, you can also install a free plugin called Pretty Links to create subdirectory-style links. One benefit of Pretty Links is that it tracks unique and total clicks, giving you more insight into what's working.

Review the results from each link every month to see which version of your copy brings in the most traffic. When you find a variation that converts well, keep it. Replace what didn't perform as strongly and test something new. Repeat the process, always refining and improving your marketing. You'll know something is working when it consistently brings in new email subscribers. If you're just starting out, don't stress about perfect numbers. Simply pay attention to which version gets more clicks or signups than the others.

THE POWER OF PERMAFREE BOOKS

The single most effective tool in growing my email list came through publishing permanently free ebooks (permafree books) across every major online retailer. In 2015, I hit a breaking point in my life where I realized that something needed to change or I had to look into getting a day job while putting my author career on hold. With the little money I had available, I hired my self-publishing coach, Jason Bracht.

One of the first things he had me do was refocus my attention on getting email subscribers, not just book sales. By focusing on building and growing a deep email list, I could have much better results with my author business.

Online retailers like Amazon merely allow authors a space to sell their wares, but they do not provide a direct connection to the customer. The solution is to capture those readers right when they buy your book or are reading a sample.

> *Side note: A huge reason I recommend authors place marketing copy for their email newsletter in the front matter is so that browsing customers might subscribe without ever spending a dime. You're essentially promoting your email newsletter for free!*

Jason instructed me to create short, easily digestible books that I could publish permanently for free. This no-cost publication attracts my ideal reader, so they have a taste of what to expect in my books.

While I'm not the biggest fan of doing work for no money, publishing permafree books is one of the few exceptions. Unlike short-term giveaways or free promotions, a permafree book stays free forever and builds long-term momentum. It's a long play that can generate revenue in several ways, including:

1. Getting new email subscribers
2. Selling more print books or audiobooks
3. Boosting backlist book sales

Authors using Kindle Direct Publishing (KDP) to publish books will know there's one slight problem with publishing a free ebook: Amazon doesn't allow this. In fact, the lowest you can price your ebook is ninety-nine cents. But the workaround is way easier than you might think.

Publish your ebook as you normally would through KDP, but set the list price higher than usual. Do not enroll your ebook in KDP Select, since that publishing model Amazon requires you to sell your ebook exclusively on Amazon. This strategy only works if your ebook is available on other retailers as well.

Next, publish your ebook through any of Amazon's direct competitors like Apple Books for Authors, Barnes and Noble Press, Google Play Books Partner Center, or Kobo Writing Life. I prefer to lean on Draft2Digital (D2D) to distribute my ebook to three of those four avenues and many other options, including libraries, subscription services, and more.

D2D will allow you to price your book as free, but they will warn you that Amazon will not allow for that. Deselect Amazon as an option since you'll distribute your book directly on Amazon via KDP's distribution.

Once your ebook is available through one of the previously mentioned competitors, it's time to gather links from every major region where your book is available.

When you have a full list of links, go into your KDP dashboard or Amazon Author Central. Select **Contact Us** and walk through the questionnaire to get email support. You'll provide them with all the details, including the ASIN (Amazon Standard Identification Number), the title, the author name, and the links. Politely ask them to price match your ebook to the other sites where it is available for free.

For example:

Please price match the following book:

ASIN: B08K21PQNS

Title: *Secrets of the Permafree Book*

Author: Dale L. Roberts

- https://itunes.apple.com/us/book/secrets-of-the-permafree-book/id1535856579

- https://itunes.apple.com/uk/book/secrets-of-the-permafree-book/id1535856579

- https://itunes.apple.com/de/book/secrets-of-the-permafree-book/id1535856579

- https://itunes.apple.com/fr/book/secrets-of-the-permafree-book/id1535856579

- https://itunes.apple.com/es/book/secrets-of-the-permafree-book/id1535856579

- https://itunes.apple.com/it/book/secrets-of-the-permafree-book/id1535856579

- https://itunes.apple.com/nl/book/secrets-of-the-permafree-book/id1535856579

- https://itunes.apple.com/jp/book/secrets-of-the-permafree-book/id1535856579

- https://itunes.apple.com/br/book/secrets-of-the-permafree-book/id1535856579

- https://itunes.apple.com/ca/book/secrets-of-the-permafree-book/id1535856579

- https://itunes.apple.com/mx/book/secrets-of-the-pcrmafree-book/id1535856579

- https://itunes.apple.com/au/book/secrets-of-the-permafree-book/id1535856579

You'll receive a standard email from Amazon explaining they reserve the right to price match and will notify you if they implement the change. Typically within one to two weeks, your title will appear with the original price crossed out.

Once your ebook is officially listed as free, promote it widely. Be clear that you're promoting the digital edition, so readers don't expect a complimentary print book or audiobook.

The same rules apply to lead magnets. The permafree ebooks you publish should tie directly to the reader's wants and needs while still honoring your author brand. Most importantly, your reader magnet should include an invitation—marketing copy—to join your email newsletter in both the front and back matter. You can get even more mileage from that free ebook by naturally mentioning one of your main books, especially the ones you want readers to discover first or the titles that best represent your work.

Much like any other publication, market and promote the book if you want to see great results. It's not enough to publish the book and pray for the best. Give the permafree book or lead magnet the same care as your other publications.

Look into free and premium book promotion services relevant to your niche when you visit my list at DaleLinks.com/BookPromos. For cash-strapped authors, sift through the options to find free book promo services specifically for free books. Set a reminder to use these no-cost services every ninety days. Since most sites promote KDP Select-enrolled ebooks on the five-day free promo, you can slip your title in with the mix. Dig even farther into that list for sites that specifically offer permafree promo services.

For authors with a marketing budget, test the premium services one at a time, so you can measure the effectiveness of a campaign. And since your book is forever free, you can test out services every day for the next year. Remember that not all premium book promo services will work for everyone, so it's important to test out the services and track the results. Do not spend money on book promotion if you have no plans to objectively review the data.

Remember, publishing a permanently free ebook means you can still monetize the print and audiobook versions. I recommend dropping the prices lower than other books in your catalogue, considering the fact that the ebook is 100% free. While you're promoting the free ebook, customers who would rather have the print or audio version will have options but will still enjoy a price break.

One of my best-performing permafree books pulls in far more print sales than ebooks. A big reason it performs so well is that I continue running Amazon ads and occasionally use paid book promotions to drive traffic to it. These promotions help keep the book visible and consistently in front of new readers. Unlike list-building giveaways where quality can be hit or miss, permafree promotions attract readers who want the book, not simply a prize.

Permafree books are essentially lead magnets on steroids. You're able to entice more readers to take your content for a spin on every major retail platform. They'll see two enticing offers to join your email newsletter within your book and will maybe pick up your backlist titles.

Should the day come that you want to fully monetize your permafree book, all you have to do is increase the price, and Amazon will follow suit. The best part is I've never had to let them know when my retail price increases on the other platforms. They see it and usually remedy it within a few days. But certainly won't hurt to put in a request if you see Amazon lagging and holding onto the free price match.

Once readers are on your list, whether they came from a permafree book, a group promo, or a website opt-in, they all enter the same journey. What matters most is how you engage them after that first interaction.

The perfect lead magnet doesn't exist, only the one that connects best with your ideal reader. Whether you use a short story, checklist, worksheet, or exclusive chapter, your offer needs to be simple to deliver, valuable to your audience, and locked with your author brand. Don't get stuck chasing the "right" format; instead, focus on creating something your readers genuinely want. Then test it, share it, and keep refining. Your email list starts with a digital handshake and grows when you consistently show up with value and respect for the people who trust you with their inbox.

CHAPTER 3:

PICK THE RIGHT EMAIL PLATFORM WITHOUT LOSING YOUR MIND

E arly in my author career, I was told without question that building an email list would be the foundation of my self-publishing business. Countless YouTubers and social media influencers insisted that email marketing not only be part of my business, but the cornerstone. They further shared that the more I invested in it—both in time and money—the more I'd get. This meant I needed a landing page host and email marketing service, both of which came at a higher cost than I could afford.

Unlike back then, now authors have options for email marketing services that won't cost them a dime and are relatively easy to learn. While authors *can* build a career without email marketing as the centerpiece, it remains one of the most powerful tools for selling more books, building a community, and having a direct connection to readers.

Yes, learning the lingo and where you should find all the right tools and analytics will take some time. Overall, email marketing services today have come a long way. You will find a few free entry-level options through services like:

- **MailerLite**: The free plan allows you to access essential tools for up to 1,000 subscribers. They're my preferred email marketing provider, but the service comes with a steep learning curve.
- **Kit**: Their free plan gives you limited access to essential tools for up to 10,000 subscribers. I've found their user interface intuitive and their premium features among the best.
- **AuthorLetter**: This relatively new company prides itself on making email marketing simple for authors. They provide free access for up to 1,000 subscribers with a few limitations.

Visit Resources at the back of the book for all the relevant links, but you do not have to settle for what I'm presenting you. It'd be selfish of me to tell you that these are the only options worth considering. But don't rush into investing in an email marketing service until you know what to look for.

My biggest issue when choosing a service was not knowing what I needed as an author compared to what some hype-bro on YouTube insisted I should have. The real problem came later. When I realized the service wasn't a good fit, I had to uproot my entire list, rebuild landing pages, and recreate all the automation sequences.

It's. A. Pain.

I'm embarrassed to admit that I've used at least six different email service providers over the past decade. That's why I lean in favor of the ones listed. Let me show you precisely what to look for and how to sort out what you don't need.

WHAT FEATURES DO AUTHORS ACTUALLY NEED?

The first essential feature to have in your email service provider is free access. If you aren't an established author with a pre-existing list or a high demand for an email newsletter, it does not make sense to spend any money. In a best-case scenario, you'll max out the subscriber limit on your free account and have to upgrade. By that time, you should understand whether you can monetize your email list. For example, MailerLite allows you to have up to 1,000 subscribers, so you'll need to figure out how you can recoup the costs once you hit 1,001 subscribers or more.

> *Side note: Don't stress, because I'll show you how to keep your subscriber volume below that threshold until you're absolutely sure you can get your money's worth.*

Don't let slick sales copy for an email marketing service lure you in. You truly need only a select few options to make the most of your efforts. Some services come with extra features that are nice to have but not essential. Here are most important features and items you'll need to consider when making a decision about email marketing providers:

- **Reporting & Analytics**: Tools for tracking your results are non-negotiables when building an effective email marketing strategy. You'll want to consider email providers that include the following:

  - **Open rate**: This metric allows you to see how many of your subscribers are opening an email. The higher the open rate percentage, the better. We'll discuss the ideal percentage later in the book.

o **Click-through rate**: This option tells you when your subscriber opens an email and clicks on a hyperlink. This allows you to identify the members of your audience who are most interested in what you're offering.

o **Unsubscribe rate**: It's nothing personal, but you still need to theorize why a subscriber changed their mind and unsubscribed. This metric will help you better analyze when you've missed the mark with your subscriber base. When this number is low, we can assume all is well...for now.

o **Bounce rate:** When a message fails to reach your subscriber due to a bad address or a full inbox, it's considered a bounce. A **soft bounce** typically means the inbox is full or the server is temporarily unavailable. A **hard bounce** happens when the address is fake or the account has been closed. Most services will automatically remove these failed contacts from your automation and campaign queues based on the type of failure.

o **Spam complaints**: Some subscribers feel they didn't sign up for your services and are being forcibly marketed to without their permission, so they mark your email as spam. This number needs to stay low as possible. To keep your email address in good standing, I highly recommend only selecting a service that provides an "Unsubscribe" option in a highly visible place in your email. It shouldn't be hard for your readers to find.

- **Landing page builder**: Don't let the term intimidate you. This is simply an intuitive tool that comes with templates or drag-and-drop website layouts where subscribers go to sign up for your email newsletter.
- **Signup forms & pop-ups**: These options are similar to the landing page builder but more flexible. You can embed signup forms or pop-ups on your website with minimal coding experience necessary. Make sure you have clear tutorials provided by the company so you don't crash your website by improperly embedding a pop-up. Side note: Pop-ups are still extremely effective for growing your email list.
- **Email automation builder**: You need at least one email automation sequence for onboarding new subscribers. Some free services will limit your number of automations, so make sure you plan accordingly.

Newbie email marketers will stop at those basic features, but the savvy author will read the fine print because with all free and premium services come limitations and special considerations. Things you need to think about:

- **Monthly email thresholds**: How many emails can you send per month on the free plan. Yeah, they're not giving you everything for free. For example, MailerLite allows up to 12,000 sends per month. It seems like a lot but becomes a challenge when you get more subscribers and want to communicate to them frequently.

- **Email support:** This might seem like a silly thing to look for, but you're going to need it at least once or twice when you're first starting out. Find the support options available and test them before you try out the platform. You'll learn whether they're attentive to your needs or there to make a quick buck.

Some email services have rules that can get your account terminated if you don't read the fine print. For example, Mailchimp has strict terms around affiliate marketing. If they detect an affiliate link in your email—even from trusted partners—they can shut down your account without warning. This is rare, but it happens. Always review your platform's acceptable use policies before running promotions.

If you're freaking out wondering if you'll get in trouble for sharing affiliate links within an account that it doesn't allow it, don't sweat it. Send people to a blog or social media post where you can place the affiliate link without violating platform rules.

Yes, even email marketing comes with rules, but I think most of you already know the big ones, like not emailing people who haven't given you permission. That's called spamming, and you do not want to do that because you can and will get blacklisted, unable to land in anyone's email inbox. It's like purgatory for email addresses.

The rest of the features are nice to have, but not mandatory for anyone new to this business. For instance, A/B split testing is a comparison tool you can use for testing out different email subject headlines. If you want to split test email subject headlines or varied content in the email, you can always send out a broadcast to half your subscriber base at a time, then compare the results a week after the campaign launches for the best results.

COMPARING TOP EMAIL SERVICES (WITHOUT PICKING A FAVORITE)

Look, I don't want to be the one telling you what service you should choose, because everyone's preferences and budgets will vary. I'm a fan of MailerLite, but I know many authors who loathe the platform. Rather than influence you into believing one platform is better than the other, here's a brief checklist to help you evaluate email marketing service providers:

- Does the free plan offer the features I need?
- Are automation tools included?
- Are there limitations on affiliate links or monetization?
- How responsive is their support team?
- What are users saying in recent reviews?

Before you fully commit to any one platform, remember that it's a pain to move from one provider to the next, so choose wisely. If you're ever lost and need a few authors to give you their thoughts, pop into my Discord community. You will get 100% honest thoughts and opinions. All referenced links are in Resources and References in the back of the book.

MAKING THE RIGHT CHOICE (AND STICKING WITH IT)

I'm sure some authors might still feel overwhelmed when shopping around for an email marketing service, despite knowing exactly what to look for. After all, how do you know if it's the right service for the long haul? You're going to know only through doing.

In 2021, I made the heavy-hearted decision to leave MailChimp as an email service provider (ESP). They changed the pricing, and I was getting gouged to have access to tools I'd had for free or as part of my paid plan for years. Well, they put an end to it, and I wasn't willing to stick it out to see if I could adjust my workflow.

I underestimated how hard it would be to switch providers. I had to rebuild everything: email automations, opt-in landing pages, and redirect links so readers landed on the correct platform instead of the one I was leaving. It sounds simple, but the process took hours. I had only used one other platform before and didn't know what I was doing. MailChimp gave me a solid system, but moving everything over proved to be a major challenge. I had to transfer all my subscribers and get the new setup running smoothly.

Enter Sendfox.

This AppSumo-owned email marketing service comes with a one-time fee, and I got an unlimited plan with up to 5,000 subscribers for $49. Wait a moment before looking it up. I love a good bargain and, even better still, one that gives me lifetime access. But some deals are too good to be true.

I got about three to four months into using Sendfox when I started noticing one concerning issue: My emails weren't going out to all subscribers despite having selected them.

My assistant and I worked with Sendfox several times to solve the problem. Somehow, they had a filtering option that suppressed inactive contacts, preventing certain messages from delivery. That meant I wasn't reaching my full list.

When I thought it couldn't get worse, it did. The reps at AppSumo and Sendfox informed me they were shutting down my account and refunding my money. Why? They told me I had sent too many emails in a month, exceeding their system's capacity.

It was a brief punch to the gut, and I held no ill will toward them. In fact, I still love AppSumo. But Sendfox was clearly not a good fit for me and my business needs.

I wasn't upset about losing my lifetime license; I own that. The reason I sent so many emails was that AppSumo offered a lifetime, unlimited-access license to my first 5,000 subscribers. The part that bothered me most was that I had to move...again!

I landed on MailerLite and happily use their services to this day.

This isn't a story to illustrate my love for MailerLite or to influence you into believing it's the best option for you. I want you to pay more attention to the fact that you only learn by doing.

Don't take weeks deciding what the best ESP is for your needs. Find a good free service and run that till the wheels fall off or until you can upgrade to premium features. Once you accumulate 1,000 subscribers or more, you're going to have a highly effective marketing tool to build your brand and sell more books.

Once you set up an account, don't wait to dig in. Explore the tools, study tutorials, and most importantly, take action. Having an email marketing service and not using it is the equivalent of having a gym membership but never exercising. You need to use that membership if you want the benefits. This is one of the biggest problems I see with some indie authors, and it's easily avoidable if you carve out time every day or week to learn about all the tools you'll be using.

Switch providers only when you absolutely have to. It's another time suck that'll take you away from other aspects of your author business and can become a slippery slope. You'll have to do everything I mentioned plus learn a new platform and where to access all its features.

You can use the principles I share on any email marketing service; you simply need to find those features within your chosen platform. The buttons might be in different places, but the core strategy remains the same. So don't wait for perfect conditions or a full understanding of every setting. Start now, take small steps, and keep learning as you go. Progress happens when you move, not when you wait.

CHAPTER 4:

THE WELCOME SEQUENCE-HOOK NEW READERS WITHOUT ANNOYING THEM

You've already figured out what your ideal reader wants and created a lead magnet to get them to sign up for your email newsletter. Now, make the strongest first impression possible by not simply welcoming new subscribers, but getting them genuinely excited about what your emails offer. What you say and deliver matter the most right after someone subscribes to your list, so you must be deliberate with what you communicate and when.

Don't worry, it's not as overwhelming or labor-intensive as it might seem. Most email services, even on their free plans, include basic automation tools that let you create a simple welcome sequence. This ensures new subscribers receive your reader magnet and an immediate sense of the value you plan to deliver. If your current provider doesn't offer this, it may be worth finding one that does. At minimum, you'll want a way to automatically greet new subscribers and deliver on your promise without having to manage the process manually every time.

Setting up automation will take some time, especially for first-time email marketers. If it's a new system for you, cut yourself some slack and be patient learning the platform. Once you have a basic understanding of email automation, join your own list to experience it from a subscriber's perspective.

If you haven't chosen your email service provider yet, don't worry. You can still learn how a welcome sequence works so you'll be ready to build it as soon as your setup is in place.

WHAT TO INCLUDE IN YOUR FIRST FEW EMAILS

The number one goal of a welcome sequence in your email automation is to set expectations, deliver high-value content, and connect with your subscribers. You don't need to overthink your message or use complicated strategies. Just be real with your readers. After all, these subscribers are interested, so do what you do best: Write for them.

Your first three emails should be all about deepening the relationship and trust you've built with your reader. Start out with a simple welcome message:

Hey, it's Dale here, and I'm glad you took me up on my *Best Seller Book Launch Checklist*. You can download your copy by clicking here.

But let's not stop there.

You might have questions about some steps, or maybe you're wondering how to actually *use* the checklist for your next launch. So, here's what I'm doing...

43

Over the next few days, I'll send you quick, bite-sized breakdowns of each section in the checklist, simple tips that clear up confusion and help you put it into action.

Here's what you need to do now to get started:

- STEP 1: Make sure you're getting my emails! Add dale@ selfpublishingwithdale.com to your safe-senders list or address book. Click here for full instructions.

- STEP 2: Let's connect! Take two seconds to subscribe to my YouTube Channel (click here), subscribe to my Substack (click here), or join my Discord (click here). These are my primary methods of communication outside of email updates, and you won't want to miss a thing.

I typically email once a week, twice max if there's something important you'll want to see. I respect your inbox, and I'm here to help, not to spam.

Till later,

Dale L. Roberts

SelfPublishingWithDale.com

P.S. Do you know the vital step in the book launch process most self-publishers skip? Well, stay tuned tomorrow, I'm going to give you the lowdown on what you *need* to start off on the right foot.

Most subscribers want their freebie right away, so don't delay. As mentioned in the previous chapter, you'll need to host your reader magnet on a cloud drive. Create a shareable link through your preferred cloud drive service to use in a clickable hyperlink within your email. Make sure you email yourself and test the download link to ensure it's working fine on your computer, smartphone, or tablet. You'll want to identify any problems before launching your offer to the public.

In that same first message, set the table and explain exactly what subscribers can expect from your content and how often they'll hear from you (see next subchapter). If you need help deciding what to write, ask new subscribers what they'd like to see in future updates. All they have to do is reply, and their message will reach you even though it was sent through your marketing platform. These readers are just arriving, so they'll often tell you what they want—and sometimes even offer tips that make your job easier.

One difficulty you'll run into is getting your email to land in the subscriber's inbox rather than the spam folder. To increase the likelihood of getting in front of your subscribers, give them instructions on how to whitelist your email. You're only a Google search away from the best instructions. If you have a website, place these instructions on an unlisted page. Send readers from the email to your website rather than to some random person's instructional blog or YouTube video.

This keeps your reader in your ecosystem while also preventing your future emails from landing in the wrong spot because of overzealous spam filters. We'll discuss other factors that contribute to this issue later, because it's not limited to whitelisting an email. In some circumstances, whitelisting your email will do you no good.

Sprinkle in a few details about where else readers can find you. This could be your website, social media, YouTube channel, or anywhere else you show up online. Most important, guide them to the one part of your business you want them to focus on. That might be your books, your store, your platform, or your newsletter archive. The welcome email is often your best-performing message, especially when paired with a strong reader magnet. Make it count.

YouTube, Discord, and Substack are my three most important avenues; you choose your preferences (if at all). Here's a good time to push your social media accounts or even showcase your backlist of books. Don't be shy! This is your time to shine, so make sure you lead with what makes the most sense for your goals.

As for length, only make the email as long as it needs to be. You'll need to experiment with what resonates most with your audience. Do they like short and punchy copy? Or would they like a long-form piece they can read in fifteen to twenty minutes? This is going to be based on your audience's expectations and your availability.

Writing a good email can feel overwhelming, especially when you're getting started. It reminds me of watching someone step into a gym for the first time. Beginners start at the bottom. But by showing up consistently, they build the muscle, strength, and endurance to keep going. You need to write at least a few dozen emails before you find your footing.

Relax and pretend you're having a conversation with one specific reader. Visualize that person, then write for them. When you're all done, close out your email with a signature.

I like to end my automation emails with an open hook—some postscript that teases an idea or concept, whetting their appetite for the next email. This open hook indirectly tells subscribers to stick around because I've got something you're going to want to tune in for.

You will still have to deliver on that promise, so in the next email in the automation sequence, open with what you hinted at in the previous email. Don't assume they'll remember; you'll need to share what you posted in the last message.

In my second message, I like to start things from scratch, pull back the curtain, and introduce myself. I share a few fun tidbits about me and sometimes a personal picture with my wife or family. My call to action is an invitation to reply to the email and share their personal stories and author business. I've gotten hundreds of emails over the years from this simple little CTA and have met some incredible people who have become cornerstones of my communities on YouTube and Discord.

How much you want to reveal about yourself is completely up to you. If you don't feel comfortable sharing pictures, that's totally fine. Heck, anyone uncomfortable on camera can find other aspects of their lives like their pets, favorite places, writing setup, and whatever their imaginations can concoct.

When you wrap things up, do the same thing in the postscript—finish with another open hook. Fiction authors could entice readers with secrets behind the writing, funny character profiles you'd never want people to see, or one of your worst blunders as a writer. Nonfiction authors can easily craft open hooks based on a pain point and teasing the upcoming email that has the solution.

In this third email, confirm your subscriber got their reader magnet with no issue. Provide the download link again so they know precisely where to get it. Sometimes, subscribers will throw out the original email and forget to download the file. This little reminder will nudge anyone who hasn't gotten it and will go a long way in showing goodwill.

Also, why go through all the trouble of creating a reader magnet if they don't read it? You hope they'll read, enjoy, and spread the word about it. In future emails, you can always follow up to see what your subscribers' thoughts were about your reader magnet. Keep the conversation going and engage your readers as collaborators. They're more invested that way.

PACING, TIMING, AND BALANCE

How often you email your subscribers depends on their expectations and your own availability. When I first got into email marketing, I thought daily emails would keep me top of mind with my readers. But that advice mostly worked for aggressive marketers trying to sell courses or hype quick wins, not for authors building long-term relationships.

In the real world, effective email marketing depends on clear, consistent communication. Start by auditing your current workload to see how much time you can realistically commit. You can build all the automation you want, but eventually new subscribers will finish that sequence. You'll need a plan to keep them engaged. Stay present in your readers' minds, but do it on a schedule that feels sustainable for you.

The X factor in all this is how long it'll take you to draft and send an email. Your first few emails can take upwards of an hour if you're overly critical about what you're writing. Some authors can easily bang out an email in minutes. For me, it takes roughly half an hour because I'm deliberate about how I craft email subject headlines and content for my subscribers to devour.

I have enough time that I can easily handle two emails per week. I've managed daily emails before, and that was highly effective in driving the unsubscribe rate. When I walked it back to fewer than three emails, I found that subscribers stuck around and, based on replies and analytics, even seemed to look forward to my emails.

At a bare minimum, email your subscriber base once per month. This brief message can go a long way toward staying relevant in your reader's world. It's often when authors feel like they've run out of things to talk about that they fall back to one email every month or around a launch time.

Do not show up only when it's convenient for you. Few subscribers will appreciate when all you're doing is emailing yet another ad for your latest werebear shapeshifter book. It's a cool book and all, but you need to lead with value first.

In *Jab, Jab, Jab, Right Hook: How to Tell Your Story in a Noisy Social World,* Gary Vaynerchuck emphasized the importance of providing value (jabs) to your audience through engaging content on social media before making a direct ask or promotional effort (right hook). Not that you should think about beating up your subscribers, but you should set them up with so much value that when you ask them to buy your latest book, it'll be the logical next step.

How could a subscriber turn you down after you've given them so much? It takes time and a lot of goodwill before you gain real traction. Some authors with large, loyal audiences no longer offer free advance copies to get reviews. Their connection with readers is strong enough that they can launch new releases at full price and still get a steady flow of reviews and sales.

Is that the right approach for every author? Not necessarily. But it shows how powerful your email list can become when you consistently deliver value. When readers feel that the relationship goes beyond a simple transaction, they become invested in you and what you create.

The day and time you send emails can also make a big difference. Most email marketing services, even free ones, let you schedule your broadcasts. Start by checking where most of your audience lives. If they are in the U.S., aim to hit their inbox mid-morning or early afternoon, ideally on Tuesday, Wednesday, or Thursday. Avoid Mondays and weekends when readers are either catching up or checked out.

Sending during those hot spots increases the likelihood of your message landing at the top of the inbox, above the clutter that collects overnight. Being that visible gives you a greater chance of engagement.

You will need to test times to see what gets you the best results. Keep in mind that you don't want to blame timing on your subscribers not engaging. The subject line drives readers to open your email and see what you have to say. We'll take a closer look at how to write effective subject lines later. That alone will not keep them coming back for more, so that's why you have to write with purpose. Make every word count so that subscribers open your emails time and again.

The best time to introduce your books is whenever you want. You don't always have to shout, "Buy my book!" in every email. In fact, the best way to promote your work is often *not* to promote it so directly. Here are a few ways to keep your book front and center without sounding like a used car ad:

1. **Share a reader review.** Grab a short quote from a fan or review site and let their words do the talking. Bonus points if it calls out something specific readers loved.

2. **Talk about an award or recognition.** If your book picked up any accolades, tell your list why it matters and what it means to you.

3. **Write about something relevant.** Pick a topic tied to your book's theme and explore it. Think blog-style emails with your book casually linked as a deeper dive.

4. **Run a Q&A.** Invite questions about your writing process or story world. Doing this reminds readers you've got a book worth asking about.

5. **Share a behind-the-scenes look** at your research or creative process. That builds connection and naturally points back to the book.

6. **Drop an excerpt.** Share a killer passage that hooks them, no hard pitch needed. If it's good, they'll want more.

7. **Mention events.** If you're speaking at a library, signing books at a con, or showing up in a livestream, tell your readers. Mentioning your appearance puts the book in focus.

8. **Feature your readers.** If someone tags you with your book, sends a fan message, or creates something inspired by your work, share it. It's social proof and engagement rolled into one. When subscribers see others featured, it encourages more people to reach out, tag you, or send their own

photos. That kind of participation builds loyalty and keeps your list active.

9. **Build a playlist.** Create and share a soundtrack that fits your book's vibe. Tie it into your story or characters for a more immersive experience.

10. **Link to related content.** If you're on a podcast or wrote a guest post that ties back to your book, share that too. Readers love seeing how your ideas show up elsewhere.

The goal here is to stay top of mind and keep your book relevant, without sounding like a broken record asking for a sale. No one likes to be sold to or feel like their relationship with you is strictly transactional. Put yourself in your subscribers' shoes. What would you want from your favorite author? How can you best embody what you would love to see?

The beauty of these ideas is to spark creativity, so don't confine yourself to what I've suggested. I'm sure you can think of other ways to share your work without pushing people for the fiftieth time to make a purchase. And if you're delivering value in the process, that's a win-win.

SCALING YOUR EMAIL LIST WITHOUT SOUNDING LIKE A ROBOT

When you're building out your automated sequence, you can schedule emails for weeks to months in advance, but you must eventually talk to these newer email subscribers. Also, it might appear weird if you're not updating automation emails now and then; some messages are timeless, but some can become outdated and stale.

I recommend reviewing your email automation sequence at least once per year. Pay attention to:

1. Which automated emails are getting the most engagement?
2. Where are you seeing a drop-off in engagement?
3. What can you do to prevent that drop-off?

Another issue to consider is when you want to start actively sending regular broadcasts outside of your automation. After all, readers expect a certain volume of emails from you based on the expectations you set from the start. Now, imagine you're getting them all warmed up and introduced to who you are. Design the email sequence to showcase every aspect of your author business and build trust in you. If you've got all the right elements I shared previously, then close out with an open hook.

Imagine if you had an email interrupt that flow. What if a new subscriber just received your welcome email, but you interrupt that flow with an email intended for a warm audience who've already gone through your automation sequence?

Enter segmentation.

Segmentation groups your subscribers based on things like what they signed up for, what they've clicked on, or what kind of books they read. Instead of blasting the same email to everyone, you send more relevant messages that match what each group cares about. It's how you talk to the right readers with the right message at the right time.

There are two beliefs about handling segmentation and automation:

1. Remove new subscribers from regular broadcast emails until they complete the sequence.

2. Include new subscribers in automation and regular broadcast emails.

Put yourself in your reader's shoes for a moment before considering the direction you wish to go. Yes, segmentation requires a few more clicks before firing off, but it is a much better approach for building a healthy long-term relationship. Without segmentation, you're bound to land in someone's email inbox way more often than you initially planned.

You have one solution for not segmenting new subscribers: Set expectations early on. Tell them you'll be emailing them frequently at first since they'll be getting some of the bonus perks up front for being a subscriber. You'll also want to inform them you want to keep everyone in the loop, so you'll be emailing them more at first.

If your automation sequence is three months, you'll probably want to tell them that. Or, if you're like prolific nonfiction author Honoree Corder you might have a year-long sequence. That's a lot, but she's straight up about it right out of the gate. Honoree tells her subscribers what to expect, so she doesn't blindside them with more emails than initially expected.

While we're still on the topic of segmentation, this is an incredible tool not simply for new readers but for your existing list. If some aren't engaging, remove them from your regular emails and send them through a targeted re-engagement campaign instead.

For instance, if I see some subscribers haven't opened my emails for a month or two, I change up my approach with the subject line and content. It's clear that there's a disconnect. While we can blame a variety of factors outside our control—cluttered email inbox, no interest in any email, life getting in the way—it's still on you to figure out how to re-engage a disengaged subscriber.

This also helps preserve your open and click-through rate percentage, improving your chances of landing in everyone's inboxes. Isolating uninterested subscribers lets you identify those truly invested in your email and those who only wanted a freebie.

Eventually, you'll have to remove inactive subscribers from your list to make way for engaged ones who are not only happy to open your emails, but excited to do it.

The whole reason for segmentation is to meet your subscribers where they are and to be intuitive enough to know when to send an email compared to when it's not a good time. Simply because you have an email list of 10,000 subscribers doesn't mean you have to talk to them all the same way.

I want you to think of the first time you meet someone. Earlier in the book, I shared how I feel email marketing is like the relationship I have with my wife. Now, think about what the conversation was like when we first met. It was probably tentative and buttoned up since we were getting to know each other. I wasn't about to overwhelm her with everything I knew and wanted to share. Instead, I paced myself almost subconsciously. It's something we all do as people.

You'll want to treat your email list with the same regard. Take it slow and don't assume that everyone subscribing to your email is on the same level as people who have known you for years.

When it comes to personalization, should you include each recipient's name? Most email marketing services make that easy. But the truth is, many people sign up using a name they don't go by. For example, someone might register as "Michael," but everyone calls him "Mike." Using the wrong name in your message can quietly suggest you're sending mass content without considering individual preferences.

I've even seen some subscribers who use goofy names or emails specifically meant for identifying trash. Some people even use a specific address for collecting junk mail. I don't expect you to weed out those folks; instead, focus on winning them over.

When you send out an email, avoid the customized name option. Instead, speak to them as you would with any friend or family member. Using someone's name when you know them well isn't always necessary, just as it isn't in emails, texts, or direct messages.

You still need to speak directly to them, but don't need to overcomplicate it with customization. A simple "you" here and there goes a long way. Again, think of your email like a conversation with a friend, and you should be good.

Mastering your welcome sequence and regular broadcasts is more than smart email marketing; it's how you build real, lasting connections with readers who want more of what you do. If you've made it this far, you've already done more than most authors will ever attempt. You've set up the foundation. Now it's time to refine, grow, and scale it.

CHAPTER 5:

BUILD SMART EMAIL SYSTEMS THAT STILL FEEL PERSONAL

T he prospect of tackling email marketing for the first time often overwhelms authors, and it's no wonder. The initial setup can intimidate beginners. After arranging everything, newbies aren't sure of what comes next. Scaling, automation, and advanced segmentation sound like you're getting ready to launch a mission to Mars. In reality, they're a combination of the right mindset and approach to growth for your email marketing.

I want to make things much simpler for you, so you can focus on the finer things of being an author (i.e., writing, promoting, watching cat videos, etc.). Though the chapter title seems imposing, it's more about making your life a lot easier with a few simple tweaks as you push forward in your email marketing efforts.

SIMPLIFY YOUR EMAIL WORKFLOWS

Keep email marketing super simple. The routine that works the best is one that meets at the crossroads of subscriber expectations and your availability. Set a realistic schedule that aims to have at least one email broadcast per month. That's the bare minimum most authors should consider because any more time between broadcasts can work against the mission of connecting with readers.

Think about it from the reader's perspective. They finish your latest book, see the opt-in, and sign up. After getting the reader magnet, they feel energized by the value you've delivered. But the momentum often dies when there's too much silence. Life gets in the way for both you and your audience. Even a four-week gap can be long enough for your name to fade. With other messages competing for their attention daily, your emails can easily slip into a forgotten pile if you're not staying in touch.

Having a monthly email minimum is going to keep you top of mind for your subscribers. When you let it go beyond one month, you're risking a disconnect with your readers.

Conversely, you don't want to send five emails a day. Some would-be experts will tell you it's okay to send daily communications, but I think you're pushing your luck by talking too much. Having too many emails can work against you, so find the perfect balance.

Once to twice per week is good, but learn what your subscriber base prefers. No email marketing guru can predict what every genre-specific reader wants; you will know what your subscribers want by simply asking.

A poll or a simple question within the email can determine subscriber preferences. Getting every one of your email subscribers to reply will be nearly impossible, so instead, focus on the data you get. If you get nothing in return, then keep pushing forward with what you can handle on a week-to-week or month-to-month basis.

The easiest way to get the job done is to schedule a block for email marketing. I close out an hour per week to work on my newsletter. After I finish composing and scheduling my next email broadcast, I analyze past campaign data and examine my automated processes to pinpoint subscriber loss and improve future retention.

Don't overthink when planning your email marketing routine. Look for an opening in your schedule and book it. Pick a specific day and time, close out your calendar, and stick to it. Should you find you're not honoring your schedule, you can always try a different time slot.

Never waste a good email. If you're sending out a weekly broadcast that delivers value, consider repurposing it later in your automation sequence. Over time, this can help you build up months of evergreen content without having to start from scratch.

You might worry that resending an email will annoy your subscribers, but here is the reality: Not every reader opens every message. By the time someone sees that content again, weeks or months may have passed. And if they do remember it, that is not a bad thing. You're reinforcing something valuable they already appreciated.

Now, do I recommend having automations booked out for over a year? No, but that's my preference, so choose what works best for you. If you run a year-long automation sequence, you're going to need to segment your audience so that you're not scaring anyone away. Keep in mind that if you have automations running at the same time as your weekly email broadcasts, it can get noisy in your subscriber's inbox.

However, if you set expectations right away, you should be fine here. Should a subscriber tire of the constant barrage of emails, you'll know it. They'll either unsubscribe or stop opening your emails altogether. Pay attention to your analytics and adjust accordingly.

The whole point of automation is to free you up to focus on what you love. If you want more time, investing in automations is a smart move. Don't expect to crank out a year of emails in one sitting. People like Honoree have built their systems over time. Start simple. Create a short sequence to welcome new subscribers during their first month. After that, you can send your regular broadcasts and gradually fold them into your automation. If you reuse past emails, make sure to review them first so the content is still accurate and relevant.

CREATE YOUR AUTHOR EMAIL TOOLKIT

I aim to spend less time on email tasks so I can focus on other parts of my business. Most people don't find email marketing as exciting as I do. In fact, some authors see it as a chore or something to avoid altogether.

The reason it can be time-consuming and rather pedestrian is because of the repetitious elements. Authors should put together their own email toolkit—a custom resource for producing email content faster.

Right off the bat, tap into an email template. Every ESP has a library of templates for you to choose from, but sometimes they're not in alignment with your brand or vision. That's okay—run with what they have and adjust on the fly. The nice part is you can alter the template and save one for future campaigns. Whenever you need to send out an email broadcast, you'll have all the elements you want in place. All you would have to do is write the content, then schedule the email.

For instance, I have three different types of emails I like to send out. Each one of them has my brand logo at the top of the message and then splits up into different sections. My custom templates include:

1. A simple email with my logo and the text.
2. A more detailed email with my logo and then three parts broken up into unique visual elements.
3. My most complex email includes an embedded video with an animated GIF, five sections, plus an interchangeable library of my books and their links.

As you build your layouts, keep accessibility in mind. Use alt text for any images, avoid sending image-only emails, and make sure your subject lines are clear and easy to read, even for screen readers or mobile devices.

Originally, I kept it dead simple. My emails were text only, and they worked fine. As I gained more traction and experience, I added elements I wanted within each broadcast. Once I had a format I liked, I saved it as a template. Then, when I was ready to send out another broadcast to my subscribers, I didn't have to fiddle with the layout of every email. And from a branding standpoint, my subscribers instantly knew who the email was from based on the recognizable graphics and content layout.

Your author email toolkit needs to include a list of winning email subject lines. For years, I've subscribed to hundreds of newsletters and studied some of the best lines that created enough intrigue for me to open the email. On a separate cloud-based document, I stored all the subject lines I liked. Later, when I was stumped for what I should use for a subject line, I'd reference this list. Sometimes, I could use the exact line, but for the most part, I'd use them as inspiration and craft my own.

Ideally, I think of two solid email subject lines for one email broadcast. From there, I'll run a split test to see what gets the best open rate. I note any insights and data for future reference and discard the subject line that failed to deliver a satisfactory open rate. Should two subject lines perform fairly equally, I'd keep them both and build variations off those winning concepts.

The other vital part of your author email toolkit is your books. Keep a complete list of your titles along with purchase links in a cloud-based spreadsheet, such as Google Sheets or Microsoft OneDrive. This list isn't for your readers, it's for you. Having everything in one place makes it easier to include links in your emails without wasting time searching for them.

I don't recommend keeping this list only on your computer. If your device crashes, you risk losing all that work. A cloud-based document is safer and gives you access no matter where you are.

While you're building that list, include a few short blurbs or bits of sales copy for each book. These will come in handy when you're promoting your books in an email. Having it ready to go will save time and help you create emails faster and with less effort.

As you gain experience, pay close attention to the redundant tasks like formatting an email, creating compelling subject lines, or getting swipe copy for a book. If you do a task more than once, consider building that into your own custom author email toolkit.

Should you still be dry on ideas, it's time to call in the help of AI. Every author has a finite amount of creative energy daily. Once they've tapped their creative well dry, what's left might not even get a single sentence fired off. This is a *huge* reason I lean on AI. While I like to keep my writing structured and stylized in my voice, some aspects I can sacrifice.

For instance, even though I've built a large list of email subject lines, I still challenge myself to come up with fresh ideas that will compel more subscribers to open my messages. That's where AI comes in. I use it to brainstorm campaign ideas, track high-performing subject lines, and write messages that keep readers engaged and taking action (whether that's buying a book, watching a video, or visiting a site).

Remember that it's not enough that you get subscribers to open your email; they must also read the content and take action when necessary. Work with AI to troubleshoot poor-performing campaigns, whether it's a low open or click rate.

I lean on AI tools like Dibbly Create and ChatGPT. Test out other options to see what's the best fit for you. Remember, the point of using AI isn't to replace your voice, but to enhance it while sparing your creative energy and time.

The best part about AI is that you can tell it exactly what you want to get out of your email campaigns. For example, here's my three-part prompt for collaborating with AI on email marketing:

Prompt:

Help me refine my email campaign to improve subject lines, flow, and click rates.

1. Generate 5–10 subject line ideas for a newsletter about [TOPIC or OFFER]. Keep them short, clear, and curiosity driven.

2. Review my draft email and suggest improvements to make it clearer, more engaging, and easier to read. Focus on maintaining my author voice and making it personal.

3. Boost the click rate by:

    1. Suggesting better placement for the call to action (CTA)

    2. Rewriting the CTA for clarity and urgency

    3. Making sure the CTA stands out but doesn't sound pushy

Here's the draft email:

[PASTE YOUR EMAIL HERE]

Finally, combine your suggestions into a single, polished version of the email that I can test.

Once you generate your prompt, return to the same thread to track results. I usually wait about a week before reviewing performance data. That gives the broadcast time to settle in readers' inboxes and provides a clearer picture of how it performed. I'm not attached to any single idea. I simply present the data and let the tool evaluate it objectively.

Whenever you're unsure, ask AI for input. I hold back my opinions to avoid influencing the response, since the model tends to mirror the user's tone and preferences. The less bias you feed it, the more neutral and useful the output tends to be.

Experiment with your own prompts. There's no ceiling here, so use the technology in the way that best supports your process. Treat it like a creative partner. You'll be amazed how much time and energy you save.

One final word of caution: Never use the raw output without reviewing and shaping it to match your voice. The tech isn't perfect, and it's not as magical as some online gurus make it sound. You're still the filter. It's your job to infuse the copy with personality, intention, and care. Readers can tell when something feels lifeless or phoned in, and that's how trust is lost.

STATS THAT ACTUALLY MATTER

We've already touched on the core email stats but now let's dig deeper into what truly matters. The five key metrics to focus on are:

1. **Open rate**: percentage of subscribers opening your emails
2. **Click rate**: percentage clicking on your links
3. **Unsubscribes**: percentage who leave your list
4. **Bounce rate**: emails that couldn't be delivered (bad addresses or full inboxes)
5. **Spam complaints**: percentage marking your email as spam

These stats matter because they're the best way for you to track the effectiveness of your campaigns. It's not enough for you to send out an email and hope for the best; you need to be mindful of these five metrics.

The open rate plays a crucial role in long-term deliverability. Email services like Gmail and Yahoo evaluate how often readers engage with your messages. When people regularly ignore your emails, it signals that your content isn't hitting the mark. Over time, this damages your sender reputation and causes platforms to deprioritize your messages in inboxes.

If your open rate tanks for too long, your emails are more likely to go to the spam folder or the "promotions" tab. You don't want that because then you'll never be able to speak directly to your audience.

But open rate is not the only factor in these email services determining the worth of your content. They focus on total engagement, which includes clicks, replies, and not marking you as spam.

The higher your open rate is, the better, but hitting 100% is nearly impossible, especially once your list exceeds 1,000 subscribers. The subject line is your biggest obstacle to reaching more of your list. Clear that hurdle, and everything else gets easier.

As of 2025, most email marketing platforms report the average open rate across all industries falls between 37% and 42%.[ii] For author newsletters specifically, it's closer to 33%, based on data from MailerLite.[iii]

Here's a general guideline to help you gauge the effectiveness of your subject lines:

- Below 30% = Needs work
- Above 30% = Decent

- 45-50% = Strong
- 50% or more = Exceptional

A higher percentage reflects a deeply loyal or niche audience that craves your content. I'm fortunate that my email newsletter has an average open rate of 54%, though it hasn't always been that way. It's taken me years to get there. These days, I'm aiming to consistently hit 60% and push even higher. You don't need to shoot for perfection, but you should always try to improve.

Once your subscribers open the email, the next best engagement metric is the click rate. Authors should include a clickable link in every email to encourage engagement. Even a postscript link to a relevant blog post can signal to inbox filters that readers want to interact with you, which helps boost deliverability.

To be clear, not all email broadcasts have to have a clickable element. Sometimes, a personal message or simple communication doesn't need a link. Most times though, you'll find that a link is essential for whatever you're communicating.

The tricky part about getting subscribers to click on your link comes down to the content you're writing. Much like books, the better your writing is, the more likely your subscribers are to take action. Discovering what resonates most with your readers comes with time and practice. Do not ignore the data.

In 2025, the average email click rate across all email marketing campaigns was 2.00%, with click rates ranging from 0.77% to 4.36%. For authors, the click rate benchmark is 2.73%.[iv] This means that if you can get nearly 3 out of every 100 subscribers to click on your link, you're on the right track.

Inevitably, some readers will unsubscribe from your email list. Don't take it personally. View it as a good sign. When someone clicks through and opts out, they create space for readers who truly want to stay connected. Others might ignore your emails and let them pile up unread. Worse, they might report them as spam, thinking that's the easiest way to stop receiving future messages.

The average email unsubscribe rate is around 0.1%, or about one in every 1,000 subscribers. For authors, that number is typically higher, closer to 0.21%.[v] This isn't something you want to increase, but some variation is normal depending on how you grow your list. If you regularly join group promotions or giveaways, your unsubscribe rate may be higher as readers leave after getting what they came for. That's not a problem as long as your engagement remains strong and your list continues to support your goals. A lower rate is better, but context matters.

Most email marketing services provide an easy-to-find unsubscribe link, usually placed at the top or bottom of the email. Leave that there. To avoid being blacklisted, your account must comply with CAN-SPAM laws. Also, if a subscriber can't easily find the link to unsubscribe, they're more likely to report spam, leading to potential problems with future deliverability.

Sometimes, though, you'll run into problems with your emails bouncing. A hard bounce occurs when a subscriber provides an invalid email address, regardless of intent. Most ESPs will filter out and remove hard-bounced emails, so you rarely have to worry about booting the offending parties. And don't go into your dashboard to troubleshoot why the email is or isn't working. Yes, some subscribers don't spell the name of their email address right, so you're stuck with whatever you have. You might think they meant to type "authordalelroberts@ gmail.com," but if they entered "athordalelroberts@gmal.com," that's exactly what ends up on your list.

That's where having a double opt-in saves you the hassle. When readers subscribe to your email newsletter, they have to confirm the subscription before ever receiving another email. This safeguard avoids hard bounces and ensures delivery to the correct inbox, providing undeniable proof of subscriber intent. Also, it separates the freebie seekers from the truly invested readers. People willing to go the extra mile to be on your email list are the exact audience you want.

Some platforms enable double opt-in by default, while others leave it optional. You can usually adjust this in your dashboard settings. Although it may slow your list growth slightly, it improves deliverability and leads to stronger long-term engagement.

Remember, a large list doesn't always equate to a good list.

The one element you can't control is the soft bounces when a subscriber's email inbox is full or their server is down. Soft bounces are going to happen, so don't stress too much if you see a few here and there.

A reasonable email bounce rate is less than 2%, but 1% is closer to an ideal number that reflects the quality of your subscriber base.

The last metric to consider is the spam rate. You want this as low as possible, because the more complaints you get, the less likely your email will reach everyone's inboxes. Keep this number below 0.1% or, again, you'll run into deliverability issues. To mitigate spam complaints, turn on double opt-in for new subscribers and provide only premium-value content in each newsletter. This means you shouldn't beat up your subs to buy your stuff all the time. That gets old real quick!

You'll face your share of challenges. Fluctuations are normal and expected. Stay focused on delivering your best with each email broadcast, and don't let setbacks discourage you.

At the same time, avoid repeating the same approach without reflection. Track your results, study the data, and refine your future campaigns to improve retention and grow your list over time.

Remember, email marketing isn't about perfection; it's about connection. You're learning to speak directly to your readers, and even if it's messy, that's exactly what they'll appreciate.

As your list grows, so can your automation. Instead of relying on a single welcome sequence, consider building out additional email paths based on subscriber behavior. For example, if someone clicks a link about your audiobooks, you can tag them and send a short follow-up series highlighting your audio catalog. If a subscriber hasn't clicked anything in a while, you can trigger a re-engagement sequence to bring them back. Over time, these systems can run on autopilot, delivering the right message to the right person at the right time without requiring more of your time each week.

Open rates, click-throughs, and unsubscribes are just one way to track your progress. While those numbers will rise and fall, the real magic is in showing up consistently, learning what resonates with your subscribers, and always striving to serve your audience better. Keep tweaking, testing, and sending those emails. Your readers are waiting for you.

CHAPTER 6:

MAKE MONEY FROM YOUR EMAIL LIST WITHOUT FEELING SALESY

I recommend that all authors start their email list with a free plan from a popular email marketing service like MailerLite, Kit, or AuthorLetter. This eliminates the financial risk of paying for a premium option too early. While the extra features may seem tempting, they aren't worth the cost until your list starts generating a clear return on investment.

For most ESPs, you're allowed to have up to 1,000 subscribers without fees. Once you pass that threshold, it's time to upgrade. The good news is that once you hit four figures in subs, you should be able to recoup the monthly investment.

Where I see some authors struggling is in fully understanding how they can make enough book sales to pay for that monthly fee, especially if they don't have a following. That's a valid concern considering how authors can profit anywhere from $1 to $7 per book. With email marketing service costs ranging from $120 per year or more, you'll need to sell 18 to 120 books to break even.

Now, that might seem scary to a lot of new authors, but it's not as daunting as you think if you know how to use your email list to sell more books and generate additional revenue. Yes, I'm saying you don't have to promote your book to make an honest living.

Monetizing your email list can be dead simple but requires some thought and preparation before sending out a single message.

SELL MORE BOOKS WITHOUT SOUNDING SALESY

I often hear from new and struggling authors that they don't want to come off as "salesy" when promoting their book. Well, that's a valid concern. You don't want to burn bridges or have your readers think less of you. When your reader subscribes to your email newsletter, they're doing it so that you can give them precisely what they're looking for. You've built a bridge between you and your ideal reader, so don't be afraid to share what you offer.

I want you to think about the last time you went to a grocery store. Were you ever put off by a product that's showcased on an endcap? Or do you think that people handing out samples are being *salesy*? Probably not, since you expect you're going to the store to buy essential items.

Throw out all that self-doubt because it should've left you a long time ago when that reader became your email subscriber. They trust you! What more evidence do you need to believe that your reader wants to hear from you and values what you offer?

One of the easiest ways to share your book without being salesy is allowing reviewers to do the talking for you. In an email broadcast, instead of sharing your latest book or time-sensitive discount, consider leading with a snippet from a review. A little goes a long way, so grab the juiciest part of a review to post in your email.

After sharing the review, give your subscribers a link to your book and then let them take it from there. You don't need any fancy tricks or specific language; you're treating it more like a casual conversation with a friend. For example:

"I couldn't put this thriller down... It kept me on edge all night!" –Amazon Reviewer

Curious to see what kept them turning pages? Check out [Your Book Title] here: [Link]. For a limited time, it'll be 99¢ on Amazon, so grab your copy now.

Here are a few ideas to help grease your creative wheels and get you promoting your book more organically:

1. **Behind-the-Scenes Peeks:** Share a brief, interesting backstory or something personal about your writing journey, and then mention the book naturally at the end. "I spent two years researching abandoned towns before writing my latest thriller. Here's what surprised me the most..."

2. **Relevant Excerpt:** Post a short, engaging excerpt or cliffhanger directly in your email, letting the story sell itself. "What would you do if you found this on your doorstep? Here's what happened next: [link]."

3. **Author Q&A or FAQ:** Address a common reader question, then naturally reference your book for additional context. "People always ask how I build tension into my stories. I

explain the full technique in Chapter 4 of [Book Title], but here's a quick tip..."

4. **"Did You Know?" Facts:** Share an intriguing, little-known fact related to your book's subject, theme, or setting. "Did you know Victorian ghosts inspired my latest mystery? Here's one creepy legend I uncovered..."

5. **Personal Connection:** Relate your book's theme or topic to a personal story or current event that resonates with your audience. "After my dad passed, writing [Book Title] helped me process grief. Here's why this chapter still hits home for me."

6. **Milestones and Celebrations:** Celebrate significant achievements or anniversaries related to your book. "It's been exactly six months since I published [Book Title]. Here's the biggest surprise so far..."

The only limits you have are your imagination and your willingness to experiment. As long as you're acting in good faith, your subscribers will be happy to hear you out. Offering value upfront boosts book sales and builds stronger reader connections.

It doesn't end there, though, because you can set up so much more through your automation. For instance, you can revive a dead book by including any of the seven options above. The best part is that it's all on autopilot. Should you see a book isn't performing as you'd like, consider producing a multi-week email sequence. Once a subscriber opens that first email or clicks your link, you can send them to the next logical sequence in a conversation about that book. In the event they don't take any action, there's no actual loss. You've at least planted the seed for readers to buy your book later.

AUTHOR COLLABORATIONS: NEWSLETTER SWAPS & GROUP PROMOS

Collaborating with other authors in your niche can move the needle in your business massively, especially through newsletter swaps and group promos.

In a newsletter swap, two authors with similar audiences team up to promote each other's books. Each one shares a recommendation, helping introduce the other to a broader, like-minded readership.

Group promos take the idea of a newsletter swap and expand it. Instead of only two authors, several join forces to promote a larger event or sale. Rather than relying on one or two subscriber lists, group promos tap into multiple author audiences at once. The rising tide can lift every boat, but you need to anchor in the right harbor to benefit.

You absolutely must work with authors you know, like, and trust. Working with people who write low-quality content or write in unrelated niches can lead to a lot of frustration, and most importantly, wasted movement.

The toughest part about collaborating with authors is finding someone willing to work with you. This means you'll have to research comparable titles in your niche, find contact information, and then do some cold outreach. You'll probably get a lot of radio silence or outright rejections. That's fine.

Keep in mind, you can always go to the next best place for collaborative outreach: author forums and online communities. Some forums and groups to consider include Wide for the Win, 20BooksTo50k, and my Discord community. Should you not find a suitable author there, ask for suggestions or recommendations. Authors can be especially helpful; all you have to do is ask.

Once you connect with an author (or several, if you're doing a group promo), agree on what you'll promote and when. Subscribe to their newsletter to understand the kind of content they send and ask them to do the same with yours so they're aligned with your messaging and timing.

The easiest way to collaborate is through premium marketing services like StoryOrigin or BookFunnel, which offer marketplaces of authors looking to collaborate. These two companies handle more than newsletter swaps and group promos, so you'll be getting more bang for your buck in other ways. What makes it dead simple is that you don't have to volley a bunch of DMs or emails to get a collaboration going. You can see what other authors are looking to promote, how many subscribers they have, and what their previous campaigns were like.

For cash-strapped authors, I recommend the hard way first. It's not fun and can sometimes feel defeating when you're getting rejections or radio silence from other authors. But if you stick to it, you'll find an author that you can work with repeatedly. As you work with other authors in your niche, you can grow together and reap the rewards from this cross-platform connection.

Here's the beauty of author collaborations: Since you're not always pushing your books, your communication feels less transactional and more conversational. You're no longer simply selling your books but offering other options outside of your content.

Many authors struggle with what to say in their emails. One simple solution is to feature another author. It gives your readers something valuable that isn't about you and introduces them to another great book or voice in your niche. Collaborations like this make content creation easier, so you can spend less time writing emails and more time focusing on your next book or marketing plan.

One critical rule: Never share your email list with another author and never ask for theirs. Each author should only send to their own subscribers. If your readers start getting emails from someone they never signed up for, you risk losing their trust. Treat your email list like gold. Keep it private, secure, and handle with care.

TURN YOUR EMAILS INTO INCOME (COURSES, COACHING, & MORE)

Believe it or not, as an author, you don't need to sell only your books to stay in business. You have so many opportunities to earn revenue beyond books, but you will have to put in additional work to make it happen.

Every new email subscriber needs to be treated with delicate precision. Think of it like a first date; you don't want to introduce yourself with an open-mouth kiss. You need to ease your way into this relationship, building trust and credibility before you ever even think about placing a peck on their cheek.

Email marketing is much the same in that you must take your time. Pay attention to your analytics. You will see a pattern of subscribers who consistently open your emails and click on your product links. This positive engagement is an indicator that they're listening with bated breath. These subscribers are your superfans—the readers who are your biggest ambassadors.

You can offer so much more than your book through one-on-one coaching or consults, deep-dive courses, or even premium memberships. For nonfiction authors, think about the next logical step for your readers to take after they've read your book and how you can best help them.

I can hear many fiction authors scoffing at this advice because it seems only applicable to nonfiction authors. This is far from the truth.

For fiction authors, you can consider other options like:

1. **Exclusive Bonus Content or Extended Scenes:** Offer exclusive epilogues, alternate endings, side stories, or deleted scenes to your newsletter subscribers or members. "Join my reader's club for bonus chapters and behind-the-scenes story insights."

2. **Early Access and VIP Reader Experiences:** Offer early access to new books, ARCs (advance reader copies), or chapter-by-chapter reveals through a premium membership. "Join my VIP readers and get my books weeks before anyone else does."

3. **Character-Focused Merchandise or Collectibles:** Sell limited-run merchandise inspired by beloved characters or story worlds, such as prints, signed editions, stickers, or clothing. "Loved the main character? Grab a signed poster or collectible bookmark set."

4. **Interactive Reader Events or Fan Q&As:** Offer access to live Q&A sessions, virtual meet-and-greets, or monthly book-club-style discussions to paying members. "Attend monthly live events to ask questions and get exclusive author insights."

5. **Audiobooks and Multimedia Adaptations:** Offer bundled audiobook discounts, narrated short stories, or immersive audio experiences to subscribers. "Prefer to listen? Members get special access to exclusive audio shorts set in their favorite book worlds."

Yes, selling more than books can be more challenging for fiction authors than nonfiction authors since the readers' expectations are much different. It's not impossible; you just have to figure out what your readers want most from you.

THE SALES FUNNEL

You'll often hear the term "sales funnel" in email marketing. At its core, it's a step-by-step process that guides readers toward becoming paying customers, without coming across as pushy or overly sales focused.

The funnel represents going from a broad audience to your most engaged, paying readers. All readers enter the funnel through your email list through your opt-in.

A high-level view of the funnel starts with subscribers receiving the free reader magnet. The next logical step is to present a tripwire or one-time offer (OTO). As soon as someone subscribes, direct them to a special deal, discount, or exclusive offer before the automated emails begin. Make sure it's enticing but doesn't require ongoing work or personal involvement on your part.

Think of the offer as a leveled-up version of your lead magnet. For instance, if you're a fitness author, you might offer a free downloadable workout program as a reader magnet. The next logical step is to offer an upgrade, like the video accompaniment or additional workouts to complement the program you already sent.

The cost of the next offer should be affordable. The process of moving people through the sales funnel is not about making millions; it's about finding who is most interested in your work. Much like the reader magnet, you'll want to have the next offer set up in advance.

I highly recommend setting it up on a *Thank You* page that pops up after a reader subscribes. Videos convert one-time offers much better than those with text. If you have the means, create a quick video explaining your limited-time deal. These days you can create a free video with Canva, CapCut, or for more experienced videographers, DaVinci Resolve. When in doubt, hire out. You can always work with a freelance platform like Fiverr to get a pro to do it for you.

Should the subscriber pass on your OTO, you'll want to segment them into a separate list and continue to build that relationship more before progressing any further. This might take a separate email sequence, or it could mean working and building trust with that subscriber before moving onto the higher-ticket offerings you have available.

The next step after the OTO is when you're ready to introduce your next best product or service. This could be your courses or memberships. You can expect to charge a higher premium than you did for the exclusive offer. Annual memberships can cost over $120 yearly (or $10 monthly), while courses range from hundreds to thousands of dollars depending on content and demand.

Your top-tier service could be coaching, consultations, or video chats during which you give your readers direct attention. Do not sell yourself short on this one; charge the highest premium since you'll be giving away your time and expertise. Much like the courses, you can command a higher price. The best way to know the pricing that suits your audience is when subscribers invest in it. If you find that you're not converting sales, consider dropping the price or offering discount codes.

Do you need to have a sales funnel to be successful as an author? No, but it certainly helps offset the costs of producing your next book or promoting your backlist. Use these earnings to cover anything in your business or personal life, your call.

I recommend starting with at least a tripwire deal when subscribers sign up. When they purchase your OTO, segment those subscribers into a VIP list where you give them advance access to all your deals, discounts, or special offers. Once you get a hang of that, progress to other options such as courses, memberships, and consultations.

AFFILIATE LINKS DONE RIGHT

Many new authors feel overwhelmed by the prospect of building even a basic sales funnel. Don't lose heart, though, because there's an even simpler way to boost your revenue and subsidize your author business: affiliate marketing.

When you like a brand, service, or product and want to get paid for sharing it, affiliate marketing is your solution. These programs will pay you a percentage of every sale while never affecting cost for the customer.

Think of the last time you recommended a friend to watch a movie you enjoyed. The local theater got all the money, while you got all the glory. Well, I don't know about you, but glory has never paid my bills! Imagine if theaters had affiliate programs so that anytime you sent someone to watch a movie, you got a cut of the ticket price.

Affiliate marketing rewards you for sharing stuff you already like, so why not tap into something your audience can appreciate and enjoy? Finding an affiliate program is dead simple.

List all companies, tools, and platforms closely connected to your brand. To find their affiliate programs, search the company name along with "affiliate program." You'll need to apply and share any required details before using their links. Once approved, you'll receive unique tracking URLs to share across your channels. Review each program's terms to honor their guidelines.

When you use an affiliate link, be sure to disclose it within your email in a conspicuous area, like at the top of your newsletter. Keep it simple and don't overcomplicate it. For example:

> *Full disclosure: This email contains affiliate links. If you purchase through them, I may earn a small commission at no extra cost to you. Thanks for your support!*

For authors who are still stumped about what they can share with their readers, here are a few examples for both nonfiction and fiction authors.

6. **Niche-Specific Products:** Fitness authors should consider workout equipment, supplements, and monthly subscription apps. Self-help authors could lean into online courses and coaching with a credible expert. Homesteading authors could share seed subscription programs, gardening tools

with any online retailer, and more. Think of your readers' primary problems, then offer them a solution through the affiliate product you happily endorse.

7. **Online Learning Platforms:** Places like Udemy, Skillshare, and Gumroad host many excellent options for online education. Explore the options and find a course or creator you can confidently stand behind and trust.

8. **Software or SaaS Products:** I've had excellent results endorsing software like ProWritingAid, Dibbly Create, Book Award Pro, and more. Find any software-as-a-service that aligns with your brand and core message, then share it with your audience.

9. **Audiobook Platforms:** Recommend audiobooks or subscriptions where readers can find your books or other niche-relevant authors.

10. **Book Box Subscriptions:** Share niche-relevant book subscription services your readers are sure to love. (i.e., OwlCrate, FairyLoot, I Love Vampire Novels, etc.)

11. **Book Retailers:** This applies to all authors—fiction and nonfiction. Amazon, Barnes & Noble, Apple, and dozens of other book retailers have affiliate programs. And yes, it's 100% legal and ethical to double-dip by sharing affiliate links to your books.

12. **Ereaders and Tablets:** Hey, your readers are going to need something to read or listen to your books on, so you might as well give them some recommendations. You get bonus points if you already own the device and can share ways you enjoy using it most.

13. **Reading Accessories:** Think about products that enhance the reading experience like reading lights, book holders, journals, or even cozy blankets.

You're limited only by what you can think of or what your audience comes to expect of you. When in doubt, ask your subscribers what brands, services, and products they like and why. You'll get a better understanding of what you can or should share that'll resonate with your reader base.

Authors can absolutely earn a living from their books, but it takes hard work, smart marketing, and steady patience. While you work toward that goal, explore other ways to monetize your author brand. If book sales are slow, income from other sources can ease the pressure and help sustain your business. As your platform grows, those extra revenue streams can scale with it and increase your overall income.

Selling books isn't your only path to profit. Your email list is more than a tool; it powers your business. Use it to promote your books, recommend trusted affiliates, or offer premium content and experiences. Start with simple steps, stay consistent, and expand as you grow confident. Your future self will thank you, and so will your readers.

CHAPTER 7:

GET YOUR EMAILS OPENED, READ, AND CLICKED

C rafting and sending an email doesn't guarantee you instant success. You'll need to account for many variables and implement some best practices so that you increase the likelihood of landing in front of your subscriber. Even with their permission to email, there's no guarantee your message will reach them.

Email services like Google and Yahoo go to great lengths to protect their account holders. Unfortunately, that puts you in a difficult position. You want to reach your subscribers, but the email services are preventing you from doing that. Sometimes, this is through no fault of yours, but at other times, you might be inadvertently triggering spam filters based on the words you're using or content you're sending.

GETTING MORE EYES ON YOUR EMAILS

We can all agree that we want to have as many subscribers opening our emails as possible, but getting to that point can be difficult. Some factors are within our control, while others depend entirely on your subscribers or their email filters.

Spam filters can be your biggest enemy in email marketing because most services have an automated vetting system that checks for spam-like qualities. This audit includes:

1. **Content Analysis:** Filters scan the text looking for suspicious words or phrases. They're also checking for excessive capitalization, punctuation, or misleading subject lines.

2. **Sender Reputation:** Email servers track a sender's reputation based on past email broadcasts. They're looking for emails marked as spam, sending volume, and how consistent their sending patterns are.

3. **Authentication Checks:** Filters verify if the email is from the sender by checking authentication methods (i.e., SPF, DKIM, and DMARC records).

4. **User Interaction:** Some filters learn from how recipients interact with emails. If they mark your email as spam, future emails have a higher chance of being filtered. However, most email marketing services will automatically unsubscribe the complainant, so your email shouldn't be going to them after even one spam complaint.

5. **Blacklists:** If your IP or domain is blacklisted for suspicious activity, email servers will outright block your content.

The last item can be intimidating; after all, who wants to be on a blacklist? You should be safe if you follow a few solid rules.

1. **Always get permission.** Never add emails to your list that you haven't received approval for. Avoid buying email lists from seedy online services or internet "gurus."

2. **Make unsubscribing dead simple.** All email service providers have this automatically built into the header or footer of every email. Double-check that this option is in place before you send your first email.

3. **Cut the spammy language.** Don't use all caps, avoid loading your subject line with exclamation points or hyperbolic titles, and always look at your content through the lens of a stranger. If your email seems over-the-top, you should probably dial it back.

4. **Clean your list.** Email subscribers will come and go, while a few of them will quietly blend into the woodwork, never opening a single email. Cut them loose or increase your odds of landing in spam folders. (More on that in the next chapter.)

Some email services like Gmail and Yahoo have systems in place to further prevent spambots and scammers from hitting your inbox. For that reason, be sure the email marketing service you select addresses authentication protocols—like SPF, DKIM, and DMARC. These items are like behind-the-scenes security checks that prove you're the real sender.

- **SPF** – Sender Policy Framework. This verifies the sender's IP address has permission to send emails on behalf of your domain.
- **DKIM** – DomainKeys Identified Mail. The sending mail server adds a cryptographic signature to prove the message came from the claimed domain and remained unchanged during delivery.

- **DMARC** – Domain-based Message Authentication, Reporting, and Conformance. It builds on the previous two protocols by telling the receiving email services what to do if an email fails those checks (i.e., reject or quarantine it) and sends you reports about suspicious activity.

Without authentication, your emails are more likely to land in spam folders or get blocked entirely. The protocols allow you to earn trust with inbox providers and protect your sender reputation.

Side Note: Every email service provider will have specific instructions on how to enable your authentication protocols, so contact support for assistance. It'll take you less than ten minutes with the right instructions. Don't let the seriousness of the term fool you; it's far easier to handle than you think.

The only hassle you have to overcome is in how you're sending your emails. If you aren't sending through a custom domain name and are simply relying on free email services like Gmail as your sender ID, you won't be able to put these authentication protocols in place.

Will you still be able to send emails through a free email service? Yes, but it's certainly going to work against your overall sender reputation. When you can afford to upgrade to a domain name-specific email, do it. Then, you can enable the authentication protocols with no issues.

Regardless of the email you send from, you'll be able to see the results in real-time from your email campaign. Always review any broadcast you send at least one week after so that you have a clearer understanding of who's opening and clicking your emails, and what subscribers are contributing to unsubscribe, spam complaints, and bounce rates. Analytics are crucial to your growth, so never take them lightly.

Anyone new to email marketing might wonder what these analytics mean and what to do with them. Let's take it one bite at a time.

IMPROVE OPEN AND CLICK RATES WITH SMALL TWEAKS

Successful email marketing relies on higher open and click rates. The more subscribers open and consume your content, the more it boosts your sender reputation. This means your broadcast is more likely to land in your subscribers' inboxes.

Open rates tell providers that recipients are interested (although privacy changes like with Apple Mail can skew this number). Clicks are stronger indicators of engagement and carry more weight since they further prove that you're delivering content in good faith. And, oddly enough, a reply or move to folders (like "Primary" in Gmail) also help signal trust.

Conversely, the opposite effect happens if many users aren't opening your emails, consistently deleting without reading, or marking as spam. Providers will filter your emails into a **Promotions** tab, or worse, toss into the **Spam** folder.

The harsh reality is you can write the best content for your subscribers, yet it won't make a difference if no one opens it. That's where the email subject line comes in. The biggest barrier to entry is how you hook your subscribers. Focus on the subject line more than any other aspect of your efforts.

Treat your email subject line as a headline in a newspaper. Your goal is to pique your subscriber's interest enough to open the email to find out more details.

Keep your title short; aim for about five to seven words that are under fifty characters. Most readers skim their emails, so you only have one shot to stand out from the rest of the inbox noise. Drafting long titles with too many words overcomplicates the process and will leave readers disinterested in a split second.

Avoid using bait-and-switch subject lines because that'll kill trust instantly. Sure, you get excellent open rates for sensationalize titles, but you'll lose your subscribers once they discover you duped them. They might stop opening future emails, unsubscribe, or even report spam. If the title doesn't fit, don't use it. A so-so subject line and average results are better than a bad, clickbait subject line that alienates your subscribers.

Don't use any spammy words like free, guaranteed, urgent, or all caps with excessive punctuation—think 💲 *URGENT!!! You WON'T Believe This FREE Bestseller Hack!!!* 💧 💧 . If you need any more examples, open your spam folder and you'll see precisely what you should *not* do.

When you lead with value or curiosity, you give subscribers a valid reason to open. Pose a question, offer a benefit, or tease a result. When in doubt, test it out. I run split tests with all my campaigns so I can adapt future campaigns for better performance. Sure, your initial emails may not perform well, but with time and practice, you'll get better results.

Tap into premium features like A/B split testing, which allows half of your audience to see one subject line, and the other half to see another. If you have a free plan, you'll have to create a split test manually by sending two separate email campaigns that each cover half your subscriber base. From there, you can extrapolate the data to determine what is or is not working in your subject lines.

Here are a few subject lines examples:

1. Suspense / Thriller – *She Disappeared. Now She's Back.*
2. Romance – *He's Her Ex. Now He's Her Boss.*
3. Fantasy – *A Crown. A Curse. One Choice.*
4. Horror – *Don't Stay in That House Tonight.*
5. Sci-Fi – *The Ship's Empty… Or Is It?*
6. Self-Help – *Stop Quitting on Your Progress*
7. Health & Wellness – *Why You're Always Tired Lately*
8. Marketing – *Email Mistakes That Kill Sales*
9. Personal Finance – *How I Saved $500 This Month*
10. Writing & Publishing – *Amazon Might Slash Your Royalties*

Should you find you're banging your head against the wall unable to craft a subject line, you have a couple options to grease your creative wheels. My first suggestion is to subscribe to any popular authors in your niche, note what they're using, and then adapt accordingly. Or consider collaborating with artificial intelligence (AI). I've found AI wildly helpful in tracking my analytics and providing me with recommendations based on past campaigns.

Feel free to use this prompt for AI:

I'm an author writing emails to my [fiction/nonfiction] readers. The email is about [brief description]. Generate 10 compelling subject lines (under 50 characters and 5–7 words max) that sound personal, spark curiosity, and avoid spammy phrasing. Each one should feel like a message from a trusted friend.

That's not to say that you should blindly trust another author or AI to give you the best subject lines. You still have to contribute your creative energy and monitor the data to adjust future campaigns based on your current results. Never abandon this ongoing process if you want to gain and maintain any momentum for your efforts.

Once you get your subscribers to open the email, your next aim should be to get them to read your content and click on what you offer. I understand that not every email is going to have a link in it, but I encourage including at least one—whether social media, your website, or any other pertinent links.

When you're initially producing the email body, write that first draft without judgment. Treat all your emails with the same care you would in writing a book. Once the first draft is done, edit the content so that it's readable, flows well, and leads to a call to action (CTA). This CTA should be for subscribers to click on a link that'll lead to your offer or provide context for your piece.

Some email marketing services offer split testing for the content, so if you're unsure of what will resonate with your audience and drive more engagement, split test it. Eventually, you'll uncover common patterns for what gets your audience to take action.

KNOW WHEN TO WORRY (AND WHEN TO IGNORE THE NUMBERS)

When you first look at your analytics, you might be unsure of what you're looking at. As mentioned in Chapter 5, authors can have an average of 3 out of 10 subscribers opening, with 4 out of 10 representing the rate across all industries. Keep your open rate as close to 100% as possible but temper your expectations with the reality that you're less likely to hit a perfect open rate the larger your email list gets. When that number dips below 30%, you're going to need to re-evaluate your approach.

With fewer than 3 out of 10 subscribers opening your emails, your sender reputation will take a hit. As noted before, lower email open rates increase the chance of being marked as spam. But it's not a one-time occurrence that'll damage your credibility. Sure, you can dip below a 30% open rate now and then; it happens to the best of us. You'll need to make up the slack in future campaigns so that you continue to show up for all readers.

When you send a message to your list, wait at least one week before gathering all the data. This gives subscribers enough time to check their inboxes and read what you sent. Ideally, they'll open it right away, but most readers aren't sitting around waiting. Give them time.

In Chapter 5, I discussed how the author benchmark for clicks is 2.73%, or about 3 out of 100 subscribers clicking on your link. The best way to increase this number is to produce high-value content that your readers have come to love in your writing. To a certain extent, you want your emails to appear genuine and from the heart. You still have to lean into copywriting—the art of writing persuasive text to promote products, services, or ideas.

The purpose of copywriting is to get readers to read text from start to finish with little friction. This content works by engaging your audience, addressing their needs, and encouraging them to take action, like buying or signing up for something of yours.

You do not need a degree in copywriting, but you should review analytics to determine how effective your content was in driving traffic through a specific link. Keep testing out and trying different placements for your link and the language guiding readers to take action. Again, split test variations to see what is more effective. With enough email campaigns, you should have enough data and can draw conclusions based on what you find.

To be clear, you should always strive to improve your open and click rates; it's never a one-and-done process. Stick with it, and you'll be rewarded over the long term. Don't let the analytics collect dust with no intervention. That's a surefire way to burn out or scare away subscribers.

Some folks will report spam when they don't know any better, aren't sure how to unsubscribe, or simply forgot about subscribing to your newsletter altogether. You can't control what subscribers will do, so lead with your best effort every time. This means that when you're writing your content, make sure you evaluate it with a critical eye.

With bounce rates, you can't control that too much beyond the double opt-in and through regular list hygiene (more on that in the next chapter). The double opt-in prevents emails with typos from slipping through the cracks. (Who knew daelroberts@gmeil. com wasn't real?) Some folks aren't doing it intentionally and are genuinely interested in your content. They, unfortunately, might've mistyped their address.

The other issue with bounces comes from full inboxes. When an inbox can't take anymore emails, it'll bounce back to you. Unless you instruct your subscribers on how to clean their email inbox to get your content, you're at the mercy of their digital hoarding.

Email deliverability might sound like a bunch of tech jargon, but it's about making sure your messages reach the people who want to hear from you. While the rules and algorithms can feel stacked against you, you're not completely powerless. You now have the tools, insights, and strategies to improve your chances of landing in front of your audience.

Don't expect perfection. Every author starts from scratch and faces challenges like unread emails or spam complaints. Keep showing up, refine your approach, and treat your subscribers like real people who chose you from the crowded online world.

Email marketing isn't about being a wizard at promotion. It's about staying consistent, adapting when needed, and building genuine connections. You've got this!

CHAPTER 8:

CLEAN UP YOUR LIST AND WIN BACK THE RIGHT READERS

E arly in my author journey, I often felt discouraged when I saw other writers in Facebook Groups or forums brag about their massive email lists. I assumed I'd never reach that level of success. But once I took the time to study and apply what I learned, I realized that asking the right questions makes all the difference.

1. What are your open and click rates?
2. How frequently do you send emails?
3. What's your niche?

Those three questions are vital to understanding an author's email marketing success. After all, anyone can grow a massive list. The hardest part is getting subscribers to open the emails, click on the offers, and come back for more.

You already know the importance of open and click rates, and now you understand the average benchmarks for each. What matters even more is how those numbers affect your sender reputation. For example, 50% of 1,000 subscribers is the same number of opens as 5% of 10,000. But only one of those lists sends a strong signal to inbox providers. A smaller list with high engagement helps your emails land in inboxes more consistently. A massive list full of cold or inactive subscribers increases your chances of being flagged as spam.

In the past when I asked authors about their list activity, I often found they'd never sent a single email. They were waiting for something, though I'm not sure what. If you want your list to work, you have to use it.

Meanwhile, those same authors are flexing their email list size, leading others to believe that it's the size of the list that counts. No, it's not! It's what you do with that list that makes all the difference. Focus on high open and click rates, not subscriber count. Those numbers are powerful indicators of an author's relationship with their audience.

The next piece of the puzzle is how often an author sends emails. If you only reach out every few months, your open and click rates won't reflect long-term success. Email marketing isn't a one-time effort; consistent communication is key to building trust and momentum. As noted earlier, aim to send at least one email per month to stay on your readers' minds. Waiting too long between messages increases the risk of being forgotten and that can lead to unsubscribes or even spam reports when you finally reach out again.

Also, the potential size of your audience depends on your niche. Fantasy romance authors might pull in far more subscribers at a faster pace than a psychological literary horror author. Self-help might get more subscribers than books about self-publishing. Context matters, folks!

A bigger challenge is keeping your audience engaged, especially as your list expands. Once you cross a certain number of subscribers, most services charge a higher monthly fee. At that point, your list should generate enough income to cover the added expense.

Oh, dear reader, don't you sweat it, because you're with one of the most frugal people you'll ever know. I worked with a free MailChimp account for years (free for up to 1,000 subscribers then) because I learned how to monitor my analytics and take action when needed.

KEEP YOUR LIST LEAN AND ACTIVE

Everyone wants a big list because it means more opportunities to market and promote their author brand. But sometimes, inactive or disinterested subscribers get in the way and drag down engagement, making it harder to measure what's working.

You already know that open rates affect sender reputation, so you're often left at the mercy of your subscribers. Some will open every time, but a select few will never open your emails, no matter what subject line you try.

We can theorize that maybe they were freebie seekers who only wanted their complimentary copy of *Dale's Guide to Werebear Hunting* or whatever lead magnet there was. They could've provided an email they never access.

Here's where I'm going to tell you the hard truth: You either have to get your subscribers either opening or unsubscribing. You simply can't afford to have a subscriber who consistently ghosts your messages.

The good news is you don't need to plead with readers to open your emails every time you send one. That approach feels awkward and needy. If a subscriber hasn't opened a single email within 90 to 180 days, you'll need to do one of two things:

OPTION 1: UNSUBSCRIBE & PURGE

For anyone who doesn't feel like doing the extra work, this option is for you. If you want to keep your open rates high, you must remove inactive subscribers from your list. And if you're using a free email marketing service, you might have to delete them to make room for new subscribers.

Before deleting anyone, consider downloading a full backup of your list. That way, you still have access to all contacts if you ever need them. For example, you might switch email services or decide to run remarketing ads through Facebook or Google. Just be sure to label the file clearly so you don't confuse outdated contacts with your active subscribers.

OPTION 2: RE-ENGAGE

The second option requires more work with some patience since you're trying to get any engagement or activity from the subscriber. Send a segmented email that focuses solely on the subscribers who haven't opened an email in the past three to six months.

Keep the subject line and email simple and to the point. All you're doing is giving a gentle tap on the shoulder. If they reply, great; they've saved their spot on your email list. If you get radio silence, it's time to part ways. Much like measuring analytics for every email broadcast, you'll want to check at least one week after you send the re-engagement email.

Here's an example:

> *Subject line: Still want emails from me?*
>
> *Body:*
>
> *Hey, it's been a while.*
>
> *You haven't opened any emails from me lately, so I wanted to check in. Do you still want to hear from me?*
>
> *If so, no action is needed. Just opening this email tells me you're still interested.*
>
> *But if I don't hear from you, I'll assume it's time to say goodbye and will unsubscribe you in about a week.*
>
> *No pressure! You're always welcome back at* DaleLinks.com/ SignUp *if things change.*
>
> *Thanks for being part of my journey.*
>
> *-Dale L. Roberts*

You'll notice I kept it simple because if this person wasn't opening any of the previous emails, what's the point in writing the next *War & Peace* for a re-engagement email? Get to the point, and readers will reward you. I've often found this email to be effective in getting a reply. Some readers have admitted to loving my content but not having the time to read it. Others love to stockpile all the emails and binge-read them later.

The simple act of opening your message signals your email marketing service to move those previously inactive subscribers back into the active group the next time you run a re-engagement campaign. On average, you'll see about 10 to 20% re-engaging with your content.[vivii]

Once you've given your inactive subscribers time to receive and read your email, if they don't re-engage, unsubscribe them and move on. You don't need additional emails and won't have to justify why you removed them.

For authors starting out, I recommend running re-engagement campaigns, especially if you have a list size smaller than 1,000. Every subscriber counts, so only keep the active ones, and cut the inactive ones loose.

Once you've seen significant growth and are bringing in hundreds to thousands of new subscribers per month, you can go with the lazier method of segmenting the inactive and unsubscribing them.

Side note: I love seeing my analytics after purging inactive subscribers because the open and click rates increase. Cutting the dead weight helps bolster those numbers and sender reputation.

WHEN LESS IS MORE

Removing subscribers can feel counterintuitive, especially when your list is small and growing slowly. But don't let the vanity metric of list size derail your mission. A smaller, more engaged list will always outperform a bloated one that drags down results. When you cut inactive readers, your open and click rates go up. That leads to better inbox placement, stronger engagement, and a clearer sense of what's working.

Not every subscriber will be either a superfan or completely checked out. Many will land somewhere in the middle. These are the people who open the occasional email, click once in a while, and quietly stay on your list. They may not be your loudest supporters, but they still find value in what you send. Keep them in mind as you evaluate your email performance.

If you're ever unsure about removing subscribers, remember this: You're not losing readers. You're making space for the ones who care.

CONCLUSION:
WHY EMAIL STILL WINS

I'm often asked in interviews what is the one thing authors should do above all else. Is it a website, blog, social media, or email marketing? Without hesitation, I answer with email marketing every time. You get a straight path to your readers without the friction you'd find on social media or a website. Are those tools effective? Sure, but in my experience, they are nowhere near as useful as an email list.

Social media can be effective, but much like when you self-publish a book on Amazon or any other retailer, you're building your presence on borrowed land. You're growing fruit in someone else's garden, and they can lock the gate at any time, leaving you with nothing.

Email marketing is different; it's a direct line to your readers. Unlike a website or blog that depends on visitors showing up, your email lands right in their inbox. You're not waiting for traffic. You're not hoping search engine algorithms favor your post. You're building a relationship on your terms, not on someone else's platform.

Email stands out because it's permission-based, personal, and consistent. Your readers chose to hear from you, which builds a stronger connection. Messages arrive in an inbox people check daily, sometimes several times. Unlike social media posts, emails don't vanish or get buried by trends. They remain until the reader opens, archives, or deletes them.

Having a list safeguards and future-proofs your author business. Instead of retailers owning that relationship, you do. Rather than social media controlling the reader connection, you do. While you have best practices to follow, that is a minor responsibility compared to everything else you need to do to gain favor with some algorithm-driven platform.

Should Amazon KDP terminate your account, you'll be ready to contact your readers immediately with the email list you've built. If a social media site goes belly up or fades into obscurity (i.e., Google+, Vine, MySpace), you can ping your subscribers to let them know where you'll be next.

From a strategic standpoint, the email list is one of the most powerful tools for building awareness of upcoming book launches, backlist bargains, and any other author-related stuff. Imagine gathering all your best and most dedicated readers in one spot and getting them excited at the same time about what they love most: your books.

You don't need a perfect email newsletter. Give it your best shot and stay consistent. I started at zero like everyone else, and for the first few years, I had no idea what I was doing. But even then, I still saw results. There's a saying that 80% of success is showing up. The truth is you don't even need to hit 80. If you show up regularly and give an honest effort, you'll make progress. You'll surprise yourself with how far you can go.

WRITE TO ONE READER, NOT A CROWD

I've often heard the advice that when you're writing the first draft of a book, do it with one reader in mind. Email marketing is much the same way. Each broadcast should be a meaningful conversation with a friend. Approach this relationship the same way you would connecting with someone close to you, with good purpose and intentions.

Cut yourself some slack if you're new to this world; it's going to take some time to get acclimated and find your way. Missing an email here or there is fine. How many times have you been upset with a friend who hasn't connected with you in a few weeks? Chances are you're going to be happy when you do see and hear from them.

Don't beat yourself up over typos or grammatical errors. Your content doesn't need to be perfect and polished. Lead with your best efforts and move forward.

Oh, and prepare yourself. You will eventually send out an email broadcast with the wrong link. Yes, it sucks, but it's a much bigger problem for you than it is for them. Send a correction email with a brief apology, then move on. No reader has ever stopped me to say, "Remember that April 2, 2010, email? You missed a typo in paragraph two, and you gave the wrong link."

Don't be mistaken—editing and polishing your content still matter. Too many typos or grammar issues can make you look careless. Fortunately, plenty of free and premium grammar tools with browser extensions can help you clean things up.

> *Side note: I love ProWritingAid and have been using their software as my first line of defense before a human editor. Check the link in the Resources chapter.*

Remember that you're speaking to another person through email. Treat that relationship with respect, deliver value, and show up consistently, and you'll win in the long term. Much like the relationship with my wife for the past decade and a half, it'll start slow and gradually grow and become stronger with time.

HERE'S WHAT YOU DO NEXT

We've gotten this far, and you're probably wondering what the next steps are after reading this book. Simple! I've got you covered here:

1. **Choose your email marketing platform.** Select a platform that offers a solid free plan, includes basic automations, provides analytics, and doesn't restrict affiliate links (if that's part of your plan).

2. **Create a lead magnet your readers will love.** Sure, you could ask for subscribers without offering anything, but your list will grow much slower. Instead, give them something valuable and relevant to your book, such as a bonus chapter, a related short story, or a helpful guide that connects to the world or topic of your main content.

3. **Build a landing page or signup form.** It's going to seem intimidating at first, but I assure you that every ESP has templates where you can select what you like best, then run with it. Don't waste time trying to make your landing page perfect. My best conversion rates happened on plain

white landing pages with a simple image, text, a signup box, and button. That's it! Never underestimate the power of simplicity.

4. **Set up a welcome email and/or automation sequence.** Oh, this is where it gets tougher. At a minimum, produce a welcome email, then figure out the rest as you go. That message should take you about ten minutes to write and automate.

5. **Email consistently.** Do it at least once per month to stay relevant. Use a simple structure like a quick personal story, a helpful insight, and a call to action. Remember to be human, not robotic. Use a voice that exudes exactly who you are; readers will love it!

6. **Monitor your key metrics.** Keep your open rate above 30% or start pruning your inactive subscribers. Split-test your emails to see what content converts into the most clicks. It's great that your readers are listening to you, but it's a lost opportunity if you can't give them a compelling reason to check out what you have to offer.

7. **Keep your list lean and engaged.** The size of your email list means diddly squat if your subscribers aren't opening or interacting with your content. Give your subscribers three to six months of inactivity before either re-engaging or removing them from your list.

8. **Grow your list strategically.** Share your email opt-in within your books, on your website, through social media, and even on merchandise (i.e., stickers, bookmarks, shirts). Avoid shady list-building tactics like buying emails or

irrelevant swaps. Collaborate with other authors only when your audiences align. It needs to make sense.

9. **Respect the readers' inboxes.** Always include the unsubscribe option in a conspicuous place. And be transparent about how often you'll send emails and what subscribers can expect. When you make a mistake, own it, apologize, and move on.

Now, if you've already started a list and you're wondering what you do next, simply start. You're in a great position if you have even one subscriber (outside of yourself, of course). Send out that first email, but this time you do it with intention. If I even gave you one spark of inspiration, use it now.

Or ask! Your subscribers will probably be happy to share what they'd like to see from you. Remember how I said to treat email like a conversation with a friend? I mean it! When I see a friend, I don't lack things to talk about. I simply talk because we know each other well enough that it's a pleasure to stop and catch up.

The most important lesson I want to leave you with is an underlying theme of my entire *Self-Publishing with Dale* series:

Take action now!

It doesn't have to be perfect. Even small, consistent actions add up to major progress. You'll soon experience a significant payoff, and not in book sales alone.

Over the years, I've received emails from indie authors who've been part of my community, sometimes for years. They've shared wins and heartbreak, breakthroughs and setbacks. What always struck me was how committed they were to their goals. If something I shared helped them along the way, I was glad to be a small part of their journey.

I'm certain you'll get that too if you stay the course, show up for your readers, and treat every email like a chance to serve, not sell. Build the kind of connection that makes someone excited to hear from you. Deliver value with consistency and care. When you do that, your email list stops being a tool and becomes a legacy. And that legacy starts with your next email. So go write it.

A SMALL ASK...

If you found *Email Marketing for Authors* helpful, I'd be incredibly grateful if you would take a moment to leave an honest review.

You can leave a review wherever you purchased or downloaded the book, or visit DaleLinks.com/ReviewEmailBook to find the quickest way to share your feedback.

Here's why your review matters:

- **It helps other authors and creators know this book is worth their time.** When someone is deciding whether or not to pick up a new resource, real feedback from real readers makes all the difference.
- **It directly supports my work.** Reviews don't affect sales rankings, but they build trust, encourage new readers to give the book a chance, and help the author community grow stronger.

Even leaving a star rating—no written review necessary—makes a huge difference.

Every bit of feedback helps authors like me continue creating resources that serve you better.

Thank you for being part of this journey, for supporting indie publishing, and for helping more authors discover the tools they need to succeed.

ABOUT THE AUTHOR

Dale L. Roberts is a bestselling author, award-winning content creator, and trusted voice in the self-publishing space. With over 50 books and 44 literary awards to his name, he's built a thriving author business by doing exactly what this book teaches: building direct, lasting relationships with readers. As the founder of the *Self-Publishing with Dale* YouTube channels, with over 123,000 subscribers combined, Dale has helped thousands of authors grow their platforms through ethical marketing, strong branding, and simple, consistent action.

From his early days struggling to get a dozen email subscribers to now reaching thousands weekly, Dale shares his hard-won insights so indie authors can skip the guesswork and start making real progress. Whether you're starting from zero or scaling an existing list, his no-fluff approach to email marketing will help you connect with readers and grow a resilient, author-first business.

Relevant links:

- Website – SelfPublishingWithDale.com
- YouTube – YouTube.com/SelfPublishingWithDale

- YouTube Podcast – YouTube.com/@SelfPubWithDale
- My Books – DaleLinks.com/Bookshelf
- Discord – DaleLinks.com/Discord
- Twitter – X.com/SelfPubWithDale
- Facebook – Facebook.com/SelfPubWithDale

WANT MORE SUPPORT LIKE THIS?

If you found this book helpful, you'll love what I send to my email subscribers. Every week, I share practical tips, real-time updates, and behind-the-scenes insights to help indie authors grow their platforms and sell more books without burning out.

Whether you're starting out or already building momentum, these emails keep you informed, encouraged, and one step ahead of the curve.

And as a thank-you for joining, you'll also get instant access to my free **Bestseller Book Launch Checklist** to help you stay focused and consistent.

Join the list and grab your checklist at **DaleLinks.com/Checklist**

SPECIAL THANKS

I'm forever in love with and grateful for my wife, Kelli. Thank you for always believing in me and standing beside my biggest, wildest projects.

Thank you to Ava Fails for sparking my passion for email marketing. I had already learned the fundamentals, but I couldn't connect the dots until I saw how she did it. I studied her subject lines, body copy, link placement, and overall strategy. Every email she sent felt like an audition to earn space in her readers' inboxes. She led with intention, and her subscribers responded by devouring everything she shared.

And of course, a huge thank you to my writing mentor and editor, Jeanne De Vita. I can't wait to dive back into our fiction projects.

Finally, a big shout-out to my beta readers, William D. Latoria and Shanon "S.D." Huston. You both bring out the best in me. Thank you.

RESOURCES

- My list of free and premium book promotion sites – DaleLinks.com/BookPromos
- MailerLite – DaleLinks.com/MailerLite
- Kit – DaleLinks.com/Kit
- AuthorLetter – DaleLinks.com/AuthorLetter
- StoryOrigin – DaleLinks.com/StoryOrigin
- ProWritingAid – DaleLinks.com/ProWritingAid

REFERENCES

i   Smith, Teddy AG. (2025 May 18). Ready, Set, Launch: Taking Your Book to the World w/ C. Martelle, D. Roberts, J. Broad & A. Bigwarfe. https://youtu.be/_mtWcm9IB9k?si=ReW4v3YedRPsWW2l

ii   Jimenez, A. (2025 April 22). Email Open Rates By Industry (& Other Top Email Benchmarks). https://blog.hubspot.com/sales/average-email-open-rate-benchmark

iii   Wildwood, L. (2025 July 10). Average Email Open Rates By Industry (2025 Data). https://bloggingwizard.com/average-email-open-rates-by-industry/

iv   Elder, D. (2025 January 13). Email marketing benchmarks by industry and region for 2025. https://www.mailerlite.com/blog/compare-your-email-performance-metrics-industry-benchmarks

v   ActiveCampaign. (2025 July 21). Email Marketing Benchmarks. https://www.activecampaign.com/glossary/email-marketing-benchmarks

vi   Okada, M. (2022 March 1). Email Benchmarks Agencies Should Use for Re-engagement Campaigns. https://agencyanalytics.com/blog/email-benchmarks-agencies-should-use-for-reengagement-campaigns

vii   Emercury. (2024 December 20). 8 Strategies for Re-Engaging Inactive Subscribers in 2025. https://www.emercury.net/blog/email-marketing-tips/8-strategies-for-re-engaging-inactive-subscribers-in-2025/

www.ingramcontent.com/pod-product-compliance
Lightning Source LLC
Chambersburg PA
CBHW070248290326
41930CB00042B/2933